BONANZA

To T.R. Barnes with gratitude

Contents

	page

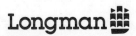

Longman Group UK Limited,
Longman House, Burnt Mill
Harlow, Essex CM20 2JE, England
and Associated Companies throughout the world.

© Longman Group Limited 1984
All rights reserved; no part of this publication may be
reproduced, stored in a retrieval system, or transmitted
in any form or by any means, electronic, mechanical,
photocopying, recording, or otherwise, without
the prior written permission of the Publishers.

First published 1984
Fourth impression 1990

ISBN 0-582-51020-1

Set in 11/13 pt Monophoto Plantin
Produced by Longman Group (FE) Ltd
Printed in Hong Kong

Acknowledgements

In preparing this book we have consulted a large number of collections of games, especially mother-tongue collections of children's games published in Europe or North America. We would like to acknowledge our debt to all the books consulted.

We would also like to thank Susan Holden and Modern English Publications for permission to reprint material from *Teaching Children*, ed. Susan Holden, MEP, 1980.

For invaluable suggestions of different kinds, our thanks are due to Gail Murphy, Director of Children's Program, Institute of North American Studies, Barcelona; to Chris Fry of the British Institute, Barcelona, and to our editors Lucy McCullagh and Alyson Lee.

Finally, Neus Valls wishes to thank her class at the Centre Educatiu Projecte, and Colin Retter to thank his class at La Salle (Bonanova) for suggesting some of the games and improving many others.

Barcelona, 1984

Introduction

What is Bonanza?

Bonanza is a collection of language games and picture cards for children aged approximately 7–12. A short section is included for younger children, aged approximately 4–6, on p. 56–59. A number of the games can also be played with older learners, including adults, e.g. *Battleships, Bingo, Busy weekend, Coffeepotting, Hangman, Happy families, Poker-face*, and others could be adapted for older learners.

Aims

The principal aims are:
1 to guide and encourage communication in English.
2 to provide reasonable coverage of teaching items.
3 to provide a collection of teaching games with the spirit of children's own games.

Why use games with children?

1 Children like them.
2 Games offer a natural context for communication between children.
3 It is sometimes difficult to persuade children to say anything at all in a foreign language. Games motivate them to speak.
4 Games provide repeated practice with teaching items. This is important for two reasons: *a)* children find it difficult to say a complete sentence in a foreign language, and *b)* they remember sentences better when they have spoken them (especially if they have spoken them in an interesting context).
5 Games have an educational value which goes beyond the foreign language lesson. They teach children about the nature of cooperation, since they cannot be played at all without it, and they encourage the development of reasoning processes, since they require a great variety of strategies.

When to use games?

Games can be used at almost any time. One important factor is the mood of the class: if they are especially restless for any reason, e.g. on windy or rainy days, they may be more interested in games than in their books.

Games can also be used to break up periods of work with books. Many teachers will be using a course book to present new language, and then using a workbook or 'activities book' to practise it. In this case, the obvious order is course book – workbook – game, with games used to break up the workbook activities.

Workbooks often have an accompanying tape of language drills, which pupils sometimes find confusing. If this happens, the teacher may prefer to select one of the items in the workbook, and play a game that includes it. Games are easier to understand, because they are a more natural activity.

Games can also be used to present new language, for example to prepare for the next unit in the course book, with the advantage that the class will understand the course book better.

Some teachers like to end a lesson with a game, if there is time. This seems to work well: the lesson gets more interesting at a point where the class are getting tired and losing concentration. Other teachers prefer to use Friday as 'games day'.

Finally, some teachers use a course book and workbook selectively, and prefer to spend more time on games and dramatic activities, because they feel pupils learn more from them.

How long do the games take?

The team competitions in which the first team to get (3)* points is the winner normally take no more than two or three minutes, but then the class want to play again. Teachers will probably be happy to play for a total of 10 or 15 minutes. One way to end the game is to say that the team winning after (10) minutes is the winner. Another possibility is to say that the first team to get (10) points is the winner.

The card games which are played in small groups are a little different. When a group have finished the game (which may be in four or five minutes, or may take much longer, depending on the game) they normally start again immediately. In real life children sometimes play a game for hours, if they are interested in it, and in the classroom they sometimes play happily for a whole lesson. What the teacher will have to decide is whether he has an alternative to offer which is equally interesting or useful. If he wants the class to stop at any time, he can shout *Stop*! The player winning at that moment is the winner.

*The brackets mean 'for example'.

1

Types of games

The games in this collection are of four different kinds:

a Traditional games

The games that children play spontaneously (playground games, card games, etc.) often have a long history; so long, in some cases, that they are traditional in many different countries. In the television age, they are played less than they used to be, but they retain a persistent appeal. Many of the games in this collection are traditional. Their status as 'classics' is a guarantee that they have a broad appeal, and they often prove among the most popular classroom games. Most of the best-known children's card games (*Happy families*, *Bluff*, *Donkey*, etc.) are included, sometimes with minor changes to adapt them to the present sets of cards.

b Games from mother-tongue collections

Some of the games are based on descriptions in European and American mother-tongue collections. Most of these are probably modern. They have one thing in common, that they were designed for one purpose only: fun.

c Foreign language games for specific teaching items

This section includes both new and previously published games which were invented to practise specific teaching items. Typical games in this category are true/false games and guessing games. The addition of cards adds variety and interest to these useful but rather limited games.

d New games

This collection contains a number of entirely new games, e.g. *Hat game* and *Poker-face*.

Why picture cards?

1 Picture cards focus children's attention, and give language practice a reality which purely verbal activities do not have.
2 Card games are fun. Holding cards seems to be a pleasure in itself, and often settles children down. In countries where there is a strong adult tradition of card games, part of the fun lies in imitating adult mannerisms, such as the way cards are put down on the table.
3 Card games have a wide appeal. They are among the most common adult games in real life, and even those children who find most children's games beneath their dignity are usually happy to play them.

4 Normally many useful language games, such as guessing games, e.g. *What animal am I thinking of?*, can only be played with the whole class, perhaps as team competitions, since the teacher has to be there to check that there is no cheating, and to fix the object of the game (e.g. the first team to get three points wins). Simple games of this kind adapt easily to card games, and the number of cards held, together with the rules and object of the game, provide the necessary framework of control. The games can then be played in pairs or groups. The question 'What animal am I thinking of?' becomes 'What animal am I looking at?' (showing the back of a card), with the advantage that when the card is turned round the guesser sees immediately if he is right.
5 Children between the ages of about 7 and 12 are fascinated by rules, and seem to accept language practice as part of the rules of the game, in much the same way as adults use fixed phrases because 'that is how the game is played'. In consequence, they are not embarrassed to speak English in card games.
6 The colour-coding of the cards reinforces the child's perception of grammatical categories. A child soon learns, for example, that 'There's some . . .' and 'There are some . . .' are phrases associated with certain colours.

The picture cards

There are 6 sets of 18 cards, giving a total of 108 (100 lexical items and 8 Jokers). The sets are: Singulars, Uncountables, Plurals, Verbs, Professions and Places.

Singulars
Cat, monkey, horse, giraffe, elephant, tiger, mouse, lion, ball, car, guitar, orange, tennis racket, camera, watch, plane, record player, +1 Joker.

Uncountables
Butter, sugar, chocolate, milk, flour, orange juice, bread, jam. There are two cards for each of these items, one showing 'a lot', the other 'not much'. There are two Jokers.

Plurals
Cats, monkeys, horses, birds, sweets, bananas, toys, records. There are two cards for each of these items, one showing 'a lot', the other 'not many'. There are two Jokers. For presentation of plural nouns, note that the cards showing cats, monkeys and horses give the three regular plurals /s, z, iz/. These cards also appear in the set of singulars.

Verbs
Cry, dance, draw, drink, eat, fly, jump, laugh, read, run, ride a bicycle, sing, swim, play tennis, watch TV, play football, write, +1 Joker.

Places
Cinema, funfair, park, school, library, home, supermarket, zoo, swimming pool, beach, baker's, butcher's, sweetshop, bookshop, football stadium, circus, museum, +1 Joker.

Professions
Policeman, scientist, astronaut, footballer, pilot, cowboy, clown, butcher, teacher, doctor, photographer, nurse, computer programmer, singer, tennis player, secretary, taxi driver, +1 Joker.

The Jokers
The Jokers are the strongest cards. They show whatever the players holding them want them to show, and they count as two cards in games in which the number of cards decides the winner.

Protecting the cards

It is not essential, but it is useful to protect the cards by covering them with adhesive plastic, as follows:
1 Cover the sheets of cards, front and back, with adhesive plastic.
2 Cut out individual cards, following the horizontal and vertical lines between cards.
3 Cut off the corners of the cards. Rounded corners last longer.

Making extra cards

There are enough cards to give three cards each to 36 children. With larger classes it will not be possible to play the small-group card games, unless the class make extra cards. To do this:
1 Give each child a small piece of paper a little smaller than the cards, to leave room for the coloured frame.
2 Tell them to draw any animal or object they wish. Tell them to draw one animal or object only, and make sure that they do the drawing vertically.
3 Choose the best drawings and stick them on cardboard.
4 Paint in the coloured frame, of the same colour as the set of Singulars.
5 Protect the cards on both sides with adhesive plastic.

Making teacher's cards (flashcards)

Although the small cards can be seen from quite a distance, it is sometimes useful to have a matching set of large teacher's cards. Perhaps the most useful sets are Verbs and Singulars. The large cards can either be copies of those sets, or can be original drawings of the same animals, objects, etc.

A good size for the cards would be around 24cm by 19cm. They can be made in the same way as the small cards described above, except that covering with plastic is less necessary, and would be expensive.

Teaching the lexis of the cards

The term lexis refers to vocabulary. The phrase 'the lexis of the cards' refers to the names of the animals, objects, etc. shown on the cards.

It is useful to teach the lexis of the cards in both the spoken and written form. This can be done as follows:
1 Show the card (e.g. the giraffe card) and ask the class to repeat the word (e.g. giraffe), perhaps twice.
2 Write the word on the board and practise the pronunciation once again. The class will find it helpful to see the card and the written word together: the card can be fixed on the board with a substance marketed in England as Blu-tack, resembling plasticine.
3 Tell them to copy the word. If they have a notebook especially for English, they can use it as a dictionary, with one letter per page. (The other end – turning the notebook upside down – can be used for sentences.)
4 Repeat with other cards. Teach four or five cards in a lesson. The index lists games which can be used to practise the lexis of the cards: see Index, **lexis**.
Note: If the children do not know the lexis of any of the cards, they can play one of the 'animal-object-person' games. See the section on these games on p. 6 in the Introduction.

Understanding the descriptions of the games

a The card symbol
The card symbol appears next to a game or variant if the cards are needed in that game.

b The language box

The main language item is given in a language box, e.g. *Happy families*, variant 2:

Language	Cards
Requests with 'Can we have some (more)?' e.g. Player 1: *Can we have some (more) chocolate, please?* Player X: *Yes, here you are.* or *Sorry, we haven't got any (chocolate).*	Uncs. and/or Plurals

The first player is described as Player 1. If he can speak to any other players as above, the other players are described as Player X and Y. If the next player is the player sitting next to Player 1, and so on around the group, players are given numbers: Player 1, Player 2, and Player 3. (In English games Player 2 is the player to the left of Player 1, but it is simplest to follow local custom.) The names Joe and Sue are used when children talk about other children in class, e.g. *Joe's wearing a red pullover*.

Brackets ( ) are used when a word is optional. In the example in the language box, the teacher decides before playing the game if he wants Player 1 to say 'more' or not, and also decides if Player X replies *Sorry, we haven't got any*, or *Sorry, we haven't got any chocolate*. An oblique stroke is used to indicate alternative words or expressions, e.g. Bring/Give me a pen. To avoid excessive use of brackets the teacher is referred to as 'he'. Player 1 is also described as 'he'. The next player (Player 2 or Player X) is referred to as 'she'.

A box showing any cards or other materials needed for a game or variant is placed next to the language box. The following abbreviations are used for cards: Uncs. = Uncountables, Profs. = Professions, and Sings. = Singulars. If there are two or more language items in the same box, they are numbered, and any sets of cards that are needed are given the same numbers, e.g. *Bingo*, Variant 3:

Language	Cards
The lexis of the cards: **1** Singular nouns, e.g. (a) giraffe **2** Uncountable nouns, e.g. bread **3** Plural nouns, e.g. giraffes	**1** Sings. **2** Uncs. **3** Plurals

c Numbers

Numbers of players and of cards are given in this section, e.g.

Numbers Groups of 3 or 4 players with (3) cards each. Brackets are used around a number to mean that the number is optional: in this case, if there are spare cards and the children ask for more than 3 each, they can have them.

Language practice before the game

Two kinds of possible language practice are suggested below: one for pupils who theoretically know the language item in the language box already, and another for pupils who have never met it before.

a Practice for pupils who know the item

If the class are already familiar with the item in the language box, they may not need any practice, but it is worth checking that they can say it acceptably. Ask them to repeat it a few times.

A model sentence or sentences on the board can also be useful. Pupils sometimes forget what they are supposed to say, and the model reminds them. Models can be used in all games in which the same sentence, or question and answer, is repeated throughout the game. This includes all the card games which are played in pairs or small groups. The model shows the part of a sentence which does not change. The part which changes is represented by a straight line. For example, if the language box includes the sentence *I've got a giraffe.*, the model shows

I've got _____

If the language box gives a sentence with a word or phrase in brackets, do not include brackets in the model. In the case of *Poker-face*, for example, the language box is as follows:

Language	Cards
Have got + the lexis of the cards, e.g. Player 1: *I've got a giraffe/an animal.* Player 2: *I (don't) believe you.*	Any set(s)

In this case, a possible model is:

I've got _____

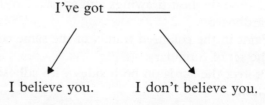

I believe you.   I don't believe you.

In the case of *Happy families*, variant 2, which was quoted earlier, the teacher first decides if he wants to include the word 'more' or not, and either includes it in his model, without brackets, or simply omits it, e.g.

Can we have some more —————, please?

Yes, here you are.   Sorry, we haven't got any.

Verbs can be replaced by a line in the same way, e.g.

What's he/she doing?   He's/She's —————ing.

The children will look at the model spontaneously when playing, so check that they can read it aloud acceptably. This can be done as follows:

1 Tell the children to follow the model with their eyes while you say it, perhaps twice. Where the model has a line for a substitution word, use a noun or verb that the children will use in the game: *He's swimming.*, *She's jumping.*, etc.
2 Ask the class to repeat it.
3 If they are still having difficulty saying a sentence, ask them to mouth it while you say it. Mouthing is the same as step 1 above, but instead of sitting passively while you speak, the children move their mouths as if they were speaking. If they are saying something incorrectly, they will see that the physical movement of their jaws does not correspond to what you are saying.

b Practice for pupils who do not know the item

If the class have not used the item in the language box before, demonstrate the game in the normal way (see below, How to demonstrate a game) but check the following points:

(i) *Understanding*: Children do not always understand a language item, even if the teacher uses mime and gesture. If they do not understand, they tend to dislike the language and become increasingly confused in class. Give them a translation of the item, or ask them to give you one.

(ii) *Pronunciation*: Children are often good at pronouncing vowels and consonants, but bad at saying complete sentences. Ask the whole class (and one or two individuals) to repeat the item. If they are having difficulty, back-chaining is very effective. Start at the end of a sentence and work back towards the beginning, taking what comes naturally, e.g. a horse – looking at a horse – I'm looking at a horse.

(iii) *The written word*: Children apparently feel the need of the written form of a word, and if they are not given it they often invent it for themselves, usually incorrectly. Write the item on the board as a model where possible, and practise pronunciation as described above. To give the class a little writing practice, tell them to copy it.

How to demonstrate a game

The best way to demonstrate a game is to play it, following the numbered steps in the Procedure section.

If the game is described as a team competition, for the whole class, it may be sufficient to explain how they win points, and who wins the game, e.g. *You get one point for each correct answer. The first team to get three points is the winner.* Or: *The team with most points at half past four is the winner.* If the game is more complicated, play it for a short time without scoring, until they understand.

If a game is described as a game for small groups (in most cases, 3 or 4 players):

1 Sit the class in a circle, if this is possible.
2 Divide the class into 3 or 4 groups, and appoint a leader in each group. Tell the leaders that they can consult other members of their group. (They will probably do this in the mother tongue.)
3 Play the game as described in the Procedure section. Take part in it yourself: you will be the leader (who shuffles and deals the cards) and Player 1 (who starts). Play with the leaders of the various groups. Explain the game as you play it: again, this will probably have to be done in the mother tongue.
4 When you see that they understand the game, make sure that they understand how it ends, and tell them to move into groups of 3 or 4 players. An alternative procedure is simply to carry on and finish the game. This has the disadvantage that individual children in the class will not have much opportunity to participate, but some teachers may prefer it, as it lets them keep control of the whole class.

Playing the game

a Team competitions

1 Appoint scorers.
   In team competitions Procedure step 1 normally says, 'Divide the class into two teams and appoint a scorer for each team.' The scorer marks the

points won, cither as simple lines: /// or in some more graphic way, such as a race to another planet:

2 Let the team consult.
In most of the team competitions, children have to say something, for example, they answer a question put by the teacher. Set a time limit for answers, e.g. 10 seconds, and let a child consult two friends before answering. This means that the child will not feel so bad if he makes a mistake.

3 Help them with the language.
In a few games, children are asked to produce sentences which they have perhaps never heard before in English. For example, in *Can I do it?* children win points for their team by suggesting things they sometimes want to do, e.g. *Can I go to the lavatory, please?* In these games, the teacher is told to help with the language if necessary.

Children find it very difficult to manipulate language: if they have learnt 'going', for example, they find it difficult to remove the 'ing' and say 'go'. The first time a game of this type is played, therefore, it will probably be necessary to help by translating the sentences they offer. If the game is played two or three times, however, it will be found that the children have remembered a lot of the language, and of course they can be encouraged to use it in class.

4 Let them be leader sometimes.
The teacher is described as the leader of team competitions. As soon as the class understand the game, however, volunteers can replace the teacher as leader.

b Small-group card games

1 Give out the cards and appoint a leader.
After demonstrating a game, tell the children to move into their groups, which are normally of three or four players. Go round the class, giving out the cards and appointing a leader in each group. The leader shuffles the cards, and deals them, and decides who starts. It is also his job to settle any disputes, if he can, and to collect the cards at the end of the game.

2 Let groups discuss a new game.
If children have not played a game before, they often spend some time discussing exactly how to play it. This is an entirely natural activity, which they do in the mother tongue. As a result of this discussion, they may introduce minor changes into the game. These changes are part of the creativity that makes group work interesting, and the teacher should only intervene if he sees that the children cannot play the game because they do not understand it. It is, in any case, a good general rule to encourage groups to find their own solutions to problems, if they can.

3 What about cheating?
Groups sometimes complain to the teacher that somebody has been cheating. Cheating can sometimes be a problem if it gets fashionable in the class, and it is probably best to take a serious line: cheating is not honest, anybody can win like that, etc.

4 Animal-object-person games.
In some of the small-group card games the players try to predict the category of a card which is face down, by saying *Animal* or *Object* or *Person*. A list of such games will be found in the index: see Index, Animal-object-person games. In these games, any card which shows a person counts as a Person card. This includes the set of Places. Any card which shows an animal counts as an Animal card. All other cards count as Object cards.

Since the language of the games is simple, they are a good way to introduce procedural language like *I'll start*. This can be written on the board and practised, with the whole class repeating:
Leader: *I'll start.* or *You start.*
Players: *It's my go/turn.* or *It's your go/turn.*
         I'm the winner!
Poker-face is a useful game for practising this, with the addition of the phrases *I/you put a card down*. With a little practice, it is possible to get the class playing entirely and fluently in English.

5 Dice games.
Some of the small-group card games also require dice: see Index, dice. (The word dice is now in general use in the spoken language as both singular and plural.)

In English dice games players have to throw the exact number to finish, and do not move at all if they throw a higher number. A slightly different ending is played in Spain. If a player needs, for example, a 2 to finish, and he throws a 5, he moves forwards two places and then backwards the remaining three places. This ending is perhaps more interesting.

If the teacher has no dice, he can get the children to make them from cardboard (opposite sides add up to seven: 6 and 1, 5 and 2, 4 and 3). Another possibility is to make a six-sided spinner out of a matchstick and cardboard.

A quicker alternative can be made from three small pieces of paper. These pieces of paper have numbers written on each side of them as if they were the opposite sides of dice: as before, opposite sides add up to seven. They are held between the knuckles, with the fingers straight, and then the fingers are opened sideways to let them fall down on to the table. The first number to reach the table is the number that counts.

To play a dice game with the whole class:

a Reduce the number of cards to nine, if necessary, to shorten the game.

b Fix the nine cards on the board with Blu-tack. Another possibility is to use a magnetboard. A magnetboard is a sheet of metal, to which magnets stick. 100 magnets can be made cheaply by cutting up a metre of magnetic strip from a hardware store. They can be placed at the top of the cards, as shown:

c Write the name of the four group leaders on small pieces of paper. Leave a little space to the right of the name, to mark the number of cards won:

d Play the game as described, with the leaders of each group (or someone else in the group) throwing the dice in rotation, in the normal way. Use the pieces of paper as markers, to mark the place of each group.

Useful phrases

After the initial explanation of a game, which will probably have to be in the mother tongue, the game should be conducted in English, so far as possible.

The following phrases may be useful; they include both teacher's language (T) and pupil's language (P).

a Introducing a game
P: Can we play a game?
T: (Yes,) O.K./All right.
T: Shall we play a game?/Do you want to play a game?/Let's play a game./Right. We're going to play a game (now).
T: I want (two) volunteers, please.

b Copying the language of the game
T: Get out your notebooks (please).
P: I haven't got a pen.
T: Ask somebody for one.
P: Have you got a pen?/Can I have a pen, please?
P: I've finished.
T: Right. Put your notebooks away.

c Moving furniture
T: Move/put your chairs against the wall. Pick them up (please).
T: Move your chairs into a circle.
T: Put your chairs back – quietly, please.

d Choosing players
Teachers sometimes use the following rhyme to choose 'volunteers', and children sometimes use it to see who starts:
Eeney, meeney, miney, mo, (ˈiːni: ˈmiːni: ˈmaini: ˈməu)
Catch a tinker by his toe,
If he hollers, let him go,
Eeney, meeney, miney, mo.

e Team competitions
T: I want two lines of five children, please. Face the front/each other/the class.
Come out to the front of the class, Joe.
O.K. You can sit down again now.
Put your hand up if you know the answer.
Hurry up! You have ten seconds (to start answering).
Whose go/turn is it?
It's your go/turn, Joe. You can consult two friends.
Keep quiet! I can't hear.
The first team to get three points wins.
We'll stop at five to four.
No. That's not (quite) right. Does anybody know the answer?
I'll offer it to Tigers.
Good. That's right. One point for/to Tigers.
We want/need a scorer (for each team).

The winners!
It's a draw!
Three all!/Three points each!
P: It's our/their go/turn.
Can I be the scorer?

f Elimination games
T: Out!/You're out!
He's still in.
You said . . . You didn't say . . . You should have said . . .

g Small-group games
T: Play in/Get into groups of three or four.
David, you go with Joe and Sue.
Joe, you're/you be the leader (of this group).
Three cards each.
Stop!/Will you stop now, please?
Will the leaders bring me the cards, please?
Leader: I'll start./You start.
P: Shuffle the cards.
It's my go/turn.
I win!/I'm the winner!
We've finished.

h Games for younger learners
In games in which one player tries to catch or touch others, the player is known as 'it' (or sometimes as 'he'):
T: Joe, you're it!
Races can be started as follows:
T: Ready, steady, GO!

Revision games

Some of the games in this collection are useful for revising previous lessons (see Index, revision games). In these games, a player is allowed to do something if he first says something correctly. In *Fish*, for example, players are allowed to propel a paper fish across the floor towards a finishing line. One way to use these games is to ask a variety of different questions from previous lessons: *What's the time? What colour's Joe's shirt?* etc. These games can also be used, however, to practise any series of questions, not necessarily for revision. You can see below how a tense of the verb – in this case, the present progressive – can be practised by asking questions about a picture card, or a child miming.

a The persons of the verb (I, you, he, etc.)
To practise the various persons of the verb, singular and plural, hold up a card from the Verbs set (in this example, the swimming card).

1 'I'. Show a child a card and tell him to mime what he sees. Ask him *What are you doing?* to elicit the reply *I'm swimming*.
2 'You'. Show a child a card and tell him to mime what he sees. Then tell him to ask another child *What am I doing?* to elicit the reply *You're swimming*.
3 'He/She'. Hold up a card, or puppets, or ask a question about a child miming: *What's he/she doing?* to elicit the reply *He's/She's swimming*. *He's got* and *She's got* can be practised with reference to a puppet or a child holding a card, e.g. *What's he got (in his hand)?*
4 We're swimming. As **1** but with two or more children.
5 They're swimming. As **3** but with two or more children.

b Other types of exchange
Most of the games in this book are described for use with 'Wh- questions', that is, questions beginning with one of the following words: what, who, where, why, when, which, and also how. Two other types of exchange can also be practised with the revision games, using cards and mime as described above.
1 Yes/No questions
Ask a question requiring a Yes/No answer, e.g.
Teacher: *Is he swimming?*
Player X: *Yes (, he is). or No (, he isn't).*
2 Negatives
Make a false statement and ask a child to correct it, e.g.
Teacher: *He's dancing.*
Player X: *No, he isn't dancing. He's swimming.*
Note: Tenses of the verb can also be practised in this way as a team competition with one point for each correct answer, as described in the game *Front of the card*.

Accumulated language

If children have been using one game too frequently with different language items, they may mix the items together and say strange things like *I've got this is an orange?* If this happens, stop using the game.

And if a child does not want to play?

It is probably not a good idea to oblige a child to play if he does not want to. The teacher should have some alternative to offer, for example copying part of a short story and illustrating it.

 **1 Auction**

Description This is a new game based on auctions. Players try to buy as many things as possible, with a limited amount of money.

Language	Cards
Money: pounds and pence, e.g. £3.50	Any set(s)

Space Normal classroom.

Numbers The whole class, in groups. The number and size of the groups is not important: there could be, for example, four groups.

Procedure

1 Divide the class into (4) groups, and appoint a leader for each group. Explain that:
   a Each group has £50 to spend at the auction. They must buy as many things as they can with it. The winning group is the group that buys most items.
   b You are going to auction (10) items. Make sure they understand that there are only (10) items.
   c The leader of each group bids for the items by raising his hand and saying a price. He can consult his group.

2 Appoint a scorer to write on the board what each group spends.

3 Auction the items, one at a time. Show a card, and give a description if you wish, e.g.
   Teacher: *This is a beautiful (nineteenth century) football. Just look at it. Lovely, isn't it? The starting price is £5. Do I hear £5?*
   Leader X: *£5.*
   Teacher: *£5, thank you, madam. £6, do I hear £6? No? Going … going … gone!* (Hits the table.) *Sold to the lady at the back for £5.*
   The 'lady' comes and collects her card, and the scorer writes on the board the money spent by the group. (If the Professions or Places sets are used tell the class to imagine that they are paintings or photographs.)

4 Auction the remaining items. Vary the starting price between 50p and £10.

5 The winning group is the group that buys most items. If two groups buy the same number of items, the group that spent less is the winner.

2 Battleships

Description Battleships is an internationally popular pair game in which one player tries to sink the other player's ships, by naming the squares on which he has placed them. There are many variants of this game. The variant shown below has the simplest language. There is another common variant in which the players name the ships: instead of saying 'Hit', they say, for example, 'Hit. Aircraft-carrier.' If the class already know the game, find out exactly how they play it, and do it the same way in English. If they name the ships, put the English equivalents (e.g. cruiser, frigate) on the board, and practise pronunciation before playing.

Language	Materials
1 Numbers 1 to 10. **2** The alphabet: letters A to J. **3** *Miss*, *Hit*, and *Hit and sunk*.	a piece of paper each

Space Normal classroom.

Numbers The whole class, in pairs.

Procedure

1 Each player draws two grids of the kind shown below:

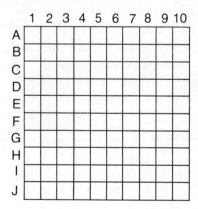

2 One grid is left blank, and players will record on it their attempts to sink other players' ships. Players put their ships on the other grid by colouring in some squares. They have one

Battleship (4 squares), two Cruisers (3 squares), three Frigates (2 squares), and four Submarines (1 square):

Battleship	▢▢▢▢	1
Cruiser	▢▢▢	2
Frigate	▢▢	3
Submarine	▢	4

Ships can be placed anywhere on the grid, horizontally or vertically, but not diagonally. Some players like to colour them, with different colours for the different types of ship. Players do not let each other see their grids.

3 The two players sit facing each other, concealing their grids.

4 Player 1 says a square, e.g. *F6*, and Player 2 looks at her grid and sees if Player 1 has hit anything. Player 2 must then respond in one of three ways: she says *Miss* if nothing is hit, *Hit* if part of a ship is hit, and *Hit and sunk* if a complete ship has been hit. So, if there are no ships on F6, Player 2 says *Miss*. Player 1 then puts a dot on F6 of his blank grid, to remind him that he has already asked about that square: ▢ .

If there is part of a ship on the square, Player 2 says *Hit* and crosses it off: ☒ . Player 1 then records on his blank grid the fact that he has hit part of something there. He draws smoke in the square: ▨ . He then has to work out which square(s) the rest of the ship occupies.

If there is a submarine on F6, the submarine is totally destroyed because it occupies only one square. Player 2 says *Hit and sunk* and crosses it off: ☒ . Player 1 records on his blank grid that he has sunk it: he puts a cross in the square: ☒ .

5 It is then Player 2's turn to try to hit something, and so on, with the two players alternating. The example below shows Player 1's record of his attempts to sink Player 2's ships.

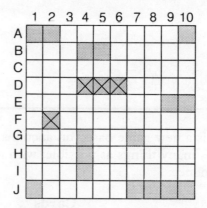

Player 2's ships

In the example above, Player 1 first said *F6*, and recorded the fact that he hit water. When it was his turn again, he said *F2*, and was lucky: he hit a submarine and Player 2 said *Hit and sunk*. His next attempt was *D4*: Player 2 said *Hit* and Player 1 at first recorded this as smoke ▨ . As he knew that there was another part of the ship somewhere he tried *C4* when it was his turn again, and he missed: Player 2 said *Miss*. Then Player 1 found the ship on D5, and D6. Player 2 said *Hit and sunk* and both crossed it out on their grids.

6 The winner is the first player to sink all the other player's ships.

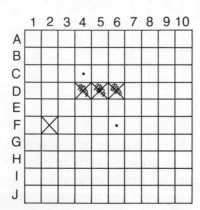

Player 1's record

3 Bingo

Description This is a well-known game of luck. The winner is the first player to cross out the numbers on his card, as described below.

Language	**Materials**
Any numbers.	a piece of paper each

Space Normal classroom.

Numbers The whole class, as individuals.

Procedure

1 Draw a bingo card and tell the class to copy it:

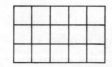

2 Tell them to put numbers, e.g. between 1 and 20, on the following squares:

Lower numbers are normally put on the left, and higher numbers on the right, to make it easier to locate numbers when playing.

3 Call out a number, e.g. 15. (Either think of numbers and keep a written record, or take numbers out of a bag). Tell the players to cross out the number if they have it on their card.

4 Call out other numbers.

5 The first player to cross out all his numbers shouts *Bingo*!

6 Check his card. If it is correct, he is the winner.

Alternative language

The alphabet

Variant 1

Players fill in the card, but have to complete the top (middle, bottom) line only.

Variant 2

Do a 'sandwich': players complete the top and bottom lines only.

With the above variants, more than one game can be played with the same card.

Variant 3

Language	Cards
The lexis of the cards:	
1 Singular nouns, e.g. (a) giraffe	1 Sings., Profs., Places
2 Uncountable nouns, e.g. bread	2 Uncs.
3 Plural nouns, e.g. giraffes	3 Plurals

Procedure

1 Show the class a set of cards. Tell them to choose nine animals, objects, etc. from the picture cards and write their names on the bingo cards, in the squares marked with a cross.

2 Shuffle the cards and put them in a pile, face down.

3 Take cards off the top of the pile, one at a time, and call out the names of the animals, objects, etc. on the cards.

4 If a player has the names on his card he crosses them out.

5 The game finishes when the first player crosses out all his names and shouts *Bingo*! Check his card.

4 Blindfolded conversation

Description This is a voice-recognition game. A blindfolded player tries to identify the voice of the person he is talking to.

Language	Materials
Any conversation of 2–4 exchanges, e.g. greetings like: Player 1: *Hello.* Player X: *Hello.* Player 1: *How are you?* Player X: *Very well, thank you.*	a blindfold

Space Normal classroom.

Numbers The whole class.

Procedure

1 Blindfold a pupil (Player 1). Turn him round a few times, and tell him to point.

2 Tell him to guess the name of the person he is pointing at when he stops (Player X). He does this by talking to her, e.g. *Hello . . . How are you?* and trying to identify the voice. Player X can disguise her voice.

3 If he identifies Player X, he can have another turn, if he wishes, or he can choose someone else to wear the blindfold. If he fails to identify Player X, it is then Player X's turn to be blindfolded.

4 If you want to make it more difficult, tell the class to change seats while the blindfolded player is being turned round.

1 Meeting people, e.g.
  Do you speak English? What's your name?

2 Addresses, e.g.
  Where do you live? I live in/at . . .

3 Directions, e.g.
  Excuse me, can you tell me the way to Park St, please?

5 Bluff

Description This is one of the classic card games. Players try to put all their cards down on the table.

Language	Cards
Animal, object, person. *I don't believe you./Let's see it.*	all sets, mixed

Space Normal classroom.

Numbers Groups of 3 or 4 players, with 3+ cards each. Players should have as many cards as possible.

Procedure

1 The leader of each group shuffles the cards and deals them. Players can look at their cards.

2 Player 1 puts a card face down on the table and says *Animal*, *Object*, or *Person*. Players do not have to tell the truth: they can 'bluff', that is, tell a lie. Let us suppose Player 1 says *Animal*.

3 Player 2 also puts a card face down. She must repeat what Player 1 said. In this example, she must say *Animal*. She may not in fact have an animal, but she must put down a card and say that it is an animal.

4 The other players put down a card, in turn, until everybody has put down a card and said *Animal*. When a player puts down a card and says *Animal*, any other player can challenge, if he does not believe him. He says *I don't believe you.*, or *Let's see it*. The player who has just put down the card then turns it over, so that everybody can see it. If the challenger is right, and the card is not an animal, the player who put it down must pick up all the cards on the table. But if the challenger is wrong, and the card is an animal, then he (the

challenger) must pick up all the cards on the table.

5 Player 2 then begins the second round. She puts down any card face down and says *Animal*, *Object*, or *Person*.

6 The first player to put down all his cards is the winner.

6 Bring me a pen

Description This game is played in kindergartens, and at adult parties (e.g. Bring me a lady's shoe). The leader asks for an object and the players try to be the first to give it to him. The basic game is principally intended to practise the lexis of classroom objects (pen, ruler, etc.). The variants also practise this lexis, but their real purpose is to practise object pronouns, e.g. *Give him a pen.*, and *Give it to him*.

Language	Materials
1 The lexis of classroom objects. 2 Pronoun 'me' as indirect object, e.g. *Bring/Give me a pen.*	a piece of chalk

Space An open area in the classroom. It can also be done with the class seated, by asking different rows of pupils for objects. The objects are passed along to the pupil on the end, who runs with them.

Numbers The whole class, as a competition for (4) groups.

Procedure

1 Divide the class into (4) groups. Stand the groups an equal distance from you. Draw a chalk line on the floor to prevent them from coming nearer. Appoint a runner in each team, to bring the objects you ask for.

2 Ask for an object, e.g. *Bring me a pen*. The first runner to bring you the pen starts making a pile of objects on the table.

3 Ask for other objects.

4 The first group to make a pile of (5) objects wins.

Alternative language

Colour adjectives, e.g. *Bring me a red pen.*

Variant 1

Language	Materials
1 *Give me/him/her/them a (pen).* 2 The lexis of classroom objects.	a piece of chalk

Procedure

Play as described in the basic game, but first stand a boy, a girl, and two children in front of the class. If you say, for example, *Give her a pen*, the runners take a pen to the girl. If you wish to make it more difficult for the class, do not point or gesture in any way when giving instructions.

Variant 2

Language	Materials
1 *Give it/them to me.* 2 The lexis of classroom objects.	a piece of chalk

Procedure

Play as described in the basic game, but:

1 Write on the board an object or objects that the class might have, but jumble the letters, e.g. clipen = pencil.
2 When a group identifies the word and finds the object, they give it to the runner, who holds it up and shouts the name of object: *Pencil!*
3 Say *Bring/Give it to me.*

Variant 3:

Language	Materials
1 *Give it/them to me/him/her/them.* 2 The lexis of classroom objects.	a piece of chalk

Procedure

Play as described in the basic game, but:

1 Stand a boy, a girl, and two children in front of the class.
2 Write on the board an object or objects that the class might have, but jumble the letters, e.g. clipen = pencil.
3 When a group identifies the word and finds the object, they give it to the runner, who holds it up and shouts the name of the object: *Pencil!*
4 Say *Give it to me/him/her/them.* The runner takes it to the appropriate person.

7
Busy weekend

Description This is a memory game. Players try to remember and repeat what the teacher has just said.

Language	Cards
Narrative (any tense) and connectors (and, but, first, then, etc.), e.g. (simple past): *I had a busy weekend. First I went to the cinema. Then I bought some sugar. I didn't buy any bread. Then I met a policeman and he asked me, 'Did you pay for this chocolate?' I said, 'Yes, of course I did . . . .'*	any set(s) mixed sets

Space Normal classroom.

Numbers The whole class.

Procedure

1 Take (10) cards.
  Show the first card – in the example above, the cinema card – and begin a narrative, based on the card, e.g. *I had a busy weekend. First I went to the cinema.* Tell the class to try to remember what you say.
2 Leave the card in view, face down. Cards can be left face down on the table or fixed to the board with Blu-tack (Introduction, p. 7), or left at various points around the room.
3 Show the rest of the cards, one at a time, and continue the narrative. In the example above, show sugar, bread, a policeman, and chocolate.
4 Repeat the whole procedure, going over the narrative again, and showing the front of the cards for a few seconds. Remind the class to try to remember everything.
5 Volunteers replace the teacher – but this time they have to say the sentences before turning the cards over. Demonstrate this with the first card: *I had a busy weekend. First I went to the cinema.* (Turn the card round to show the cinema.) *Then I . . .* Let a volunteer continue.
6 If the volunteer makes a mistake, he is replaced by another volunteer, until somebody does the complete narrative.

8 Can I do it?

Description This is a simple but useful game, based on sentences beginning with the words *Can I …?*

Language	Materials
Requesting permission, e.g. Player X: *Can I go to the lavatory, please?* Teacher: *Yes, O.K./All right.*	

Space Normal classroom.

Numbers The whole class, as a team competition.

Procedure

1 Ask the class to think of things they sometimes want to ask permission to do.

2 Give each team 10 seconds to offer a sentence, e.g. *Can I go to the lavatory, please?* It may be necessary to accept sentences in the mother tongue, and translate them.

3 Give one point for each sentence offered. Since the sentences will all be of practical use in the classroom, they can be written on the board as they are suggested, and after the game the pupils can practise saying them, and copy them into their books.

4 The team or group with most points after (10) minutes wins.

Alternative language

1 Offering, e.g.
Player X: *Shall I clean the board?/I'll clean the board.*

2 Asking somebody to do something, e.g.
Player X: *Can you switch the light on, please?*

9 Chang, Cheng, Ching, Chong, Chung

Description This is a mother-tongue game known as 'The Emperor's Vase'. A player has to name another player without breaking any of the rules given below in Procedure, step 1.

Language	Materials
The simple past, e.g. Teacher: *Who broke the Emperor's vase? … Cheng did.* Cheng: *No, I didn't./I didn't break it … Chang-Chang did.*	

Space Normal classroom – if possible, in a circle.

Numbers This game goes well with a group of about ten. When numbers reach twenty or more, it takes rather a long time to finish, half an hour, perhaps, and it may be better to play with two teams and set a time limit (see Variant).

Procedure

1 Write the following rules on the board, for reference:

> a) You must answer in 5 seconds.
> b) You mustn't name the previous speaker.
> c) You mustn't name a child who is out.

2 Explain to the class that they are in the court of one of the Emperors of ancient China. Give them their names. The first five are called Chang, Cheng, Ching, Chong and Chung. Then come Chang-Chang, Cheng-Cheng, etc., followed by Chang-Chang-Chang, Cheng-Cheng-Cheng, etc. If necessary, have the Honourable Chang, and use all the names again. If that is not sufficient, have the Very Honourable Chang, and even the Very, Very Honourable Chang.

3 Start the game by saying *Who broke the Emperor's vase? … Cheng did.*

4 Cheng replies *No, I didn't. Chang-Chang did.*

5 Chang-Chang also denies it: *No, I didn't. Chung did.* The game is passed in this way from one child to another. Refer to the rules on the board. If a

small group of friends are monopolizing the game, divide the players into two teams and introduce the rule that the game can only be passed once to a player in the same team. It must then be passed to the other team; players who do not do this are out. Keep a record of who is out, but do not let the players do this.

6 Players are progressively eliminated for breaking the rules.

7 When a lot of players are out, and getting restless, speed the game up by introducing the following rule: players are out for making a mistake of any kind when speaking, e.g. stumbling over a word: Ch . . . Chang.

8 The winner is the last player still in the game when all the others have been eliminated. The game may have to end with two players as winners, if both are good.

Alternative language

With a little thought, this game can be used for a great many language items. For example: the Emperor's court is too big, and the Emperor, as an economy measure, wants to dismiss some of his followers, starting with the silliest ones.

Teacher: *Who's silly? . . . Cheng's silly!*

Cheng: *I'm not silly! Chang-Chang's silly!*

Variant

This is a team competition for a large class.

1 Divide the class into two teams, and set a time limit, e.g. 15 minutes.

2 Introduce the rule that the game can only be passed once to a player in the same team.

3 Play as above. Keep a record of who is out, and which team he is in, in two columns.

4 The team with most players still in after (15) minutes is the winner.

10 Clock

Description This is an adaptation of a traditional Spanish game. Players reproduce the time by pretending to be the hands of a clock.

Language	Materials
The time – hours and minutes.	a piece of chalk

Space An open area in the classroom. Enough space is needed to draw a clock on the floor, with the numbers inside it. The circle can be small if necessary, e.g. 1.5 m in diameter.

Numbers The whole class, in two teams.

Procedure

1 Draw a clock on the floor:

2 Stand the teams in two equal rows. One team represents the 'big hand' and the other team represents the 'little hand' of the clock.

3 Call out a time, e.g. *Ten past seven*. The players on the end of each row reproduce the time by standing at appropriate points of the clock, as shown above.

4 Give one point to each player who stands in the correct place.

5 The winning team is the team with most points at the end of the game, which can be whenever the teacher wishes, e.g. after 10 minutes.

11 Coffeepotting

Description This is a mother-tongue game which is often played as a foreign language game for adults. Players try to guess a verb by asking questions.

Language	Materials
1 Wh- questions, e.g. what, when, where, why, who + how.	
2 Simple present and present progressive, e.g. *Do you/Does everybody coffeepot? Are you coffeepotting now?*	

Space Normal classroom.

Numbers The whole class.

Procedure

1 Put the following on the board, for reference:

Do you
Does everybody } coffeepot?

Are you coffeepotting now?

When
Where
Why
How } do you coffeepot?

Other questions that can be added, optionally, are:

What
Who } do you coffeepot with?

Other tenses can also be added, optionally, e.g.
When did you coffeepot last?
How long have you been coffeepotting?

2 Go outside the room with a volunteer and choose a verb, e.g. swim.

3 Go back to the classroom. Stand the volunteer in front of the class.

4 Explain that he has chosen a verb like dance, jump, etc. The verb is a secret, and they have to guess it. They can ask questions: instead of the verb, they say 'coffeepot'. Explain that this is a nonsense word, and instead of coffeepot they could say any meaningless word e.g. blop. Refer to the questions on the board, which they can use if they wish, in any order they wish.

5 Anyone who wants to ask a question puts his hand up.
Player X: *Do you coffeepot?*
Volunteer: *Yes (, I do).*
Player Y: *Does everybody coffeepot?*
Volunteer: *No (, they don't).*

6 The class carry on asking questions until somebody guesses the word. If they keep guessing verbs instead of asking questions, make them ask a question before each guess. Be careful with the question *How?* If a player asks *How do you coffeepot?* the volunteer may demonstrate by

moving his arms – and this will make it too easy. If you include *How?* ask for a purely verbal response, e.g. *With my arms.*

7 The player who guesses the verb is the winner, and replaces the volunteer.

Variant

In this variant the class know the word and the volunteer tries to guess by asking the questions. This can be more fun for the class, but it is less fun for the volunteer, who sometimes feels uncomfortable.

12 Dance of the ostriches

Description This is a game from a mother-tongue collection. It is known as The Cock Fight, but the present title produces a less violent game! There are two players. Each player tries to see what number the other player has on his back.

Language	Materials
Low numbers.	2 clothes pegs (or adhesive tape)

Space An open area in the classroom, or the playground.

Numbers The whole class, in 2 teams.

Procedure

1 Divide the class into two teams.

2 Select one child from each team and stand them facing each other, ready to begin the dance.

3 Attach a piece of paper showing a number to the back of each child, using the clothes pegs. Put the children's hands behind their backs.

4 Give a point to the first child who says the number on the other child's back.

5 Then it is the turn of the next children in the teams.

6 The first team to get (3) points is the winner.

Alternative language	Materials
1 The alphabet. 2 Colours.	2 clothes pegs coloured paper, or the written word

13 Do you like your neighbours?

Description This is a popular mother-tongue game. Players try to change seats, but there are not enough chairs, and one player is left standing in the middle.

Language	Materials
Teacher: *Do you like your neighbours?* Player X: *No, I don't.* Teacher: *Well, change them.* Player X: *All right. Sue and Dave!*	

Space Enough for the players to sit in a circle.

Numbers The whole class.

Procedure

1 Sit the class in a circle and stand in the middle.
2 Ask any pupil (Player X) if she likes her neighbours: *Do you like your neighbours?* Explain the word, and explain also that here it means the person on her left and the person on her right.
3 Player X replies *No, I don't.* If she wants to say *Yes*, because she does like them, insist that the rules of the game are that she must say *No!*
4 The teacher says *Well, change them.* and Player X says *All right.* and names any two other players, e.g. *Sue and Dave!*
5 The 'old neighbours' and the 'new neighbours' all change seats as quickly as they can. While they are doing this, the teacher sits in one of the vacant chairs – if he can! This leaves one of them without a chair.
6 The pupil without a chair stands in the middle and asks any other pupil *Do you like your neighbours?* At first it may be necessary to help the child in the middle with this question.

Variant 1

Language	Materials
1 Animal lexis. 2 *I can/can't see/hear an elephant.*	

Procedure

1 Sit the class in a circle.
2 Explain that the children are going to be animals. They tell you which animal they want to be. If the children use all the animals they know, the same animals can be used again, so that there are several lions, tigers, etc. This also produces a very good game, because more children are actively involved.
3 Write the names of the animals on the board.
4 Stand in the middle with a microphone (real or imaginary) and give a radio commentary.. Near the beginning of the commentary say how many animals you are going to talk about (in this example, three) e.g. *Good (morning). This is (Joe Smith) of the BBC, London. I'm in the zoo in (Barcelona). I can see (3) animals. Over there I can see a lion. And over there I can see a tiger. I can't see an elephant, but I can see a camel.*
5 When the last animal is named (in this example, the third i.e. the camel) all the animals named change places. N.B. The elephant did not count, because it was not seen.
6 The game continues in the same way as the basic game, with one player left standing in the middle. That player begins his own radio commentary – with help from the teacher if necessary.

Alternative language

Simple past, with days or months, e.g. *I went to the zoo on Sunday. I didn't have much time. I only saw (3) animals. I saw . . .*

If the next child says Monday, and the next says Tuesday, and so on, the days of the week can be practised.

Variant 2

Language	Materials
Present progressive, e.g. *I'm drawing an elephant.*	

Procedure

1 As in Variant 1, all the class sit in a circle pretending to be animals, but this time there is a child, Sue, in the middle. Sue has no chair. She is pretending to draw animals.

2 The teacher interviews her, e.g.
Teacher: (with microphone) *Good morning. This is (Joe Smith) of the BBC, London. I'm talking to you today from the zoo in (Barcelona). With me is (Sue Jones). Sue's drawing (4) animals. What animals are you drawing, Sue?*
Sue: *I'm drawing a lion, a tiger, an elephant, and a giraffe.*

3 As in the basic game, the animals change places, and Sue tries to sit on one of the chairs.

4 The child left standing in the middle takes Sue's place and pretends to be drawing.

5 The teacher interviews her, as above.

6 Other verbs which can be used instead of drawing are looking at, painting and taking a photo of. After a time, hand over the microphone to a volunteer, and help him with the language if necessary.

14 Dominoes

Description This is an adaptation of the well-known game of dominoes. Players try to put down all their 'dominoes' (in this adaptation all their cards).

Language	Cards
Animal, object, person. *I pass.*	all sets, mixed

Space Normal classroom.

Numbers The whole class, in groups of 3 or 4. 3+ cards per player.

Procedure

1 Write on the board the values of the cards, and the order in which they have to be put down:

> Person – 3 points
> Animal – 2 points
> Object – 1 point
> Person . . .

2 The leader shuffles the cards and deals them. Players look at their cards and sort them into Animal, Object and Person categories.

3 The first player puts down a card, face up, saying which category it is, e.g. *Animal*. He can begin with any category he likes.

4 Refer to the board, and explain that cards have to be put down in the order in which they appear in that column, that is: person-animal-object-person etc.

5 The second player puts down the next card, if she has it, again face up. In this example, she puts down an object card and says *Object*. If she does not have the card, she says *I pass.*

6 It is then the turn of Player 3, and so on, around the group. The line of cards can only move in one direction. Players cannot use the other end of the line, as they can in the real game of dominoes.

7 The winner is the first player to put down all his cards. Second and third place are decided by the cards which the others are left holding. Refer to the board: a person is 3 points, an animal 2, and an object 1. The player holding the least number of points comes second.

15 Donkey

Description This is a popular card game in many countries. In some places it is called 'Old Maid'. It takes a little time to organize, but is worth it because it is great fun. Players try to pass a certain card, the 'donkey', to somebody else, because they do not want to be left holding it at the end. The player holding the card at the end is a donkey.

Language	Cards
Take/choose/pick a card.	Pairs of cards from all sets, mixed, & Jokers

Space Normal classroom.

Numbers Groups of 3 or 4 players (4 is a good number), with 3 cards per player.

Procedure

1 Show the class the Joker. Explain that the player left holding it at the end of the game is a donkey,

and the other players will chant *Donkey! Donkey!*

2 Tell them that they will play in groups of four, so far as possible.

3 Show them the cards needed for each group: for groups of four – the Joker and six pairs of cards (animal, object or person cards); for groups of three – the Joker and four pairs.

4 The leader shuffles the cards, and deals them out. In groups of three, each player has three cards. In groups of four, the leader gives himself four cards and the others three each.

5 All players look at their cards and put down any pairs they have, face up.

Take a card.

6 Player 1 holds out his cards face down, spread out like a fan, and says to Player 2 *Take/choose/pick a card.* Player 2 turns to Player 3 and offers him a card, and so on around the group. Players make pairs as soon as they can, and put them down on the table, face up. If a player only has one card, he gives it to the next player and, says *Here you are.* He is not out of the game, because somebody will give him a card later.

7 The player left holding the Joker when all the other cards are down on the table is the donkey. The others chant *Donkey! Donkey!*

I6 Draw a man

Description This is a simple drawing competition.

Language	Materials
Any lexis.	2 pieces of chalk

Space Normal classroom.

Numbers The whole class, in 2 teams.

Procedure

1 Select two children, one from each team, and give them a piece of chalk each.

2 Tell them to draw something on the board, e.g. *Draw a giraffe.*

3 Give them (30) seconds. The one who does the best drawing, in the teacher's opinion, wins a point for his team. The first team to get (3) points wins.

Alternative language

Post-modification, e.g.
Draw a giraffe looking at a helicopter.

Variant

Language	Materials
Prepositions of place, e.g. *Draw a man. Draw a tree to the left of the man. Draw a bird on the man's head.*	2 pieces of chalk

Procedure

Play as in the basic game, except that the point goes to the child who has followed the instructions most accurately. If both children have drawn accurately, give the point to the better artist.

I7 Earth, air and sea

Description This game is played in many different countries. In the original game, players say the name of an animal that lives on land (or in the air, or in the sea).

Language	Materials
Numbers Any two lexical sets, e.g. animals/objects clothes/parts of the body	a ball

Space Normal classroom, preferably with the children in a circle, around the walls if necessary. It can also be played in the playground.

Numbers The whole class.

Procedure

1 Write the following rules on the board, in the mother-tongue if necessary:

You are out if you:
a) do not speak in 3 seconds.
b) say a word of the wrong category.
c) say the same word as the previous child.

---

2 Stand the children in a circle and give them numbers.

3 Start the game by calling out a number, e.g. *18*. Child number 18 puts his hand up and says *Here!*

4 Throw him the ball and say *Animal* or *Object* (or whatever lexical sets you are practising).

5 The child catches the ball and then has three seconds to say the name of, for example, an animal. Refer to the rules on the board. Players can have three lives (that is, be out three times), to keep everyone in the game.

6 If the child says the name of an animal in three seconds, it is his turn to call out a number, throw the ball, and say *Animal or Object*. If he does not name an animal in three seconds he loses a life, and must throw the ball back to the teacher.

7 The game ends whenever the teacher wishes. There are no winners. To make the game more difficult, introduce the rule that a player is out if he names an animal or object that has been named before.

18 Father Carbasser

Description This is a traditional game in many countries. The version described below is that played in Catalonia. Players have to say a simple phrase containing two numbers (e.g. From 5 to 8). They must say it quickly and correctly, and cannot say the number of a player who is out.

Language

Numbers 1 to (20) and prepositions from, to, e.g.
From 5 to 8.
When Father Carbasser came back from the war he brought (5) pumpkins.

Materials

Space Normal classroom. If possible, the children should be seated in a circle.

Numbers The whole class.

Procedure

1 Write the following rules on the board:

You are out if you:
a) do not speak in (3) seconds.
b) make a mistake when you speak.
c) say the number of somebody who is out.

---

2 Give each child a number.

3 Start the game by saying *When Father Carbasser came back from the war he brought (5) pumpkins.* (In fact, any other sentence will do equally well; the only important thing is that it has a number in it).

4 Child number 5, in this example, chooses another number, e.g. 8, and says *From 5 to 8*. Refer to the rules on the board. Explain that rule b) means that they must say the words 'from' and 'to' correctly, and must say their own number first: 5, in this example.

5 If a child breaks one of these rules, he is out. Make a note of his number, but do not let the class do this.

6 If child number 5 says *From 5 to 8* correctly, it is then the turn of child number 8. Number 8 then thinks of another number, e.g. 17, and says *From 8 to 17*. It is then the turn of number 17, and so on.

7 A child in difficulties has an escape route. He can say *Father Carbasser* instead of a number, e.g. *From 17 to Father Carbasser*. The teacher then starts the game again, as at the beginning.

8 The game normally ends with two winners, because two players do not normally make a mistake.

 **19 First letter**

Description This game is based on identifying the first letter of the animals, objects, etc. on the cards.

Language	Cards
1 The alphabet. **2** The lexis of the cards.	any set(s)

Space Normal classroom.

Numbers The whole class, as a team competition. 3+ cards per child.

Procedure

1 Divide the class into two teams and appoint a scorer for each team.

2 Give out the cards, from any sets, 3+ cards per child.

3 Go through the alphabet from the beginning. As you say each letter, children hold up cards which they believe to begin with that letter. Jokers can be used once only. They must then be handed over to the teacher.

4 Give one point for each correct card, and take one point off for each mistake.

5 The team that gets most points is the winner.

 **20 Fish**

Description This is a mother-tongue game which is very amusing visually. Players propel a paper fish towards a finishing line.

Language	Cards/Materials
Revision of questions, e.g. *What's the time?* *What colour's Joe's shirt?* etc.	paper scissors (optional) any set(s)

Space An open area in the classroom, or the playground.

Numbers Groups of any size – or representatives of groups. Ideally, the child propelling the fish

should be able to turn round and consult all the other members of his group.

Procedure

1 Divide the class into (six) groups and tell each group to draw and cut out a fish. The fish can be of any size. Sometimes it is the biggest fish that wins, and sometimes it is the smallest.

2 Draw two parallel lines, some two metres apart, on the floor. Place the group leaders behind the lines, as shown:

3 Explain that the object of the game is to propel the fish across the far line. Demonstrate how they can propel their fish by striking the ground behind it with a folder, newspaper, etc. If noise is a problem, a player can put his fist on the ground, rest his chin on his fist, and propel the fish by blowing hard. He must not move his head to follow the fish.

4 Ask a player on one side a question, e.g. *What's the time?* (Optionally, questions can refer to cards, e.g. *What's he doing?*) If the player answers correctly, he can propel the fish. If he does not answer correctly, he can be made to repeat the correct answer, and can then propel his fish, but with a smaller object, or, if he is blowing, he can blow from a greater distance.

5 Ask a player behind the other line a question, and so on, alternating from one side to the other.

6 Players cannot touch the fish, unless the fish are blown sideways out of the area of the game. Part of the fun of the game is the way the other side's fish are blown backwards.

7 The winning fish is the first to cross one of the lines. The other players play for second and third places. To keep everybody in the game, the fish that have finished can turn round and start again from the line they have just crossed. Players cannot improve their final positions, but they have the fun of moving their fish.

Alternative language

1 Possessives and comparatives, e.g.
Teacher: *David, look at Joe's fish and Sue's fish. What can you say?.*
David: *It's bigger.*/*Joe's fish is bigger than Sue's.*

2 Superlatives, e.g.
Teacher: *David, what about Ann's fish? What can you say?.*
David: *It's the fastest.*

Variants

There are many possible variants of this type of game. Anything that is visually interesting can be used for a team competition, for example, building a tower of matchboxes on the back of a child's hand (one child representing each team holds a tower), or throwing balls that stick on a target, or throwing rings around sticks (with a different number of points for each stick), or bouncing a ball into a wastepaper basket, or taking penalties at football with a goalkeeper from the other team, etc. Some of these may be more suitable for the playground than the classroom. See also 'Paper aeroplane competition', p. 43.

 **21 Flick**

Description This is a new game which requires some luck and some skill (memory). Players try to collect as many pairs of cards as possible.

Language	Cards
Animal, object, person.	all sets, mixed

Space Normal classroom.

Numbers Groups of 3 or 4 players, with 3 cards each.

Procedure

1 The leader shuffles the cards and deals. Players can look at their cards.

2 Players hold their cards spread out, showing the back of the cards. The cards should not be too close together.

3 Player 1 looks at his cards and sees what he needs to make a pair of Animal, Object or Person cards. If he already has a pair, (e.g. two animal cards) he ignores it, because in this game pairs are made of one card from the hand, and one card won from another player. If he needs an animal, he flicks (thumb and first finger) the card of any other player (X) and says *Animal!*

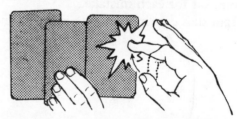

4 Player X turns the card round, so that everybody can see it. If it is not an animal, it is then Player X's turn to flick any card, belonging to any other player. If it is an animal, Player 1 takes it, and puts down his pair of animal cards. He can then flick any other card, belonging to any player, and can carry on doing this until he makes a mistake. Whenever he can, he makes a pair and puts it down.

In this game, a player does not have to have an (animal) to ask for one. If he remembers the cards held by other players he can carry on winning them all, until he makes a mistake, making pairs when he can. It is useful to have as many cards as possible, to make pairs later.

5 The game ends when no more pairs can be made.

6 Scoring: three points for each pair held, and one point for each single card. The player with most points is the winner.

22
Foreign shopper

Description This is a miming game from a mother-tongue collection. Players try to guess what a 'foreign shopper' is miming.

Language	Materials
The language of shopping, including the lexis of goods in shops, e.g. *Can I have that ball, please? Can I have 200 g of butter/some of that butter, please? Can I have 100 g of sweets/some of those sweets, please? How much is that ball?*	

Space Normal classroom.
Numbers Whole class.
Procedure
1 A volunteer role-plays a foreign visitor who doesn't speak the language. The visitor must first say what kind of shop he is in. If he is in a supermarket he must say which department.
2 The rest of the class are shop assistants. They try to guess the exact words he is trying to mime, e.g. *Can I have that ball, please?*
3 The first one who says the complete sentence replaces the foreign shopper.

 23
Front of the card

Description This is a very common and simple way to use picture cards: the teacher shows the front of a card and asks a question. It can be made into a competitive game by giving one point for each correct answer.

Language	Cards
Any question referring to the cards, e.g. Teacher: *What's he doing?* Player X: *He's swimming.*	any set(s), e.g. Verbs

Space Normal classroom.
Numbers The whole class, optionally as a team competition.
Procedure
1 Hold up the front of a card and ask any child (Player X) a question, e.g. *What's he doing?* Player X replies, e.g. *He's swimming.*
2 If this is done as a team competition, let Player X consult two friends.
3 Give one point for each correct answer. The first team to get (3) points is the winner.

Variant 1
1 Write the children's names on pieces of paper and put them all in a bag or hat. Alternatively, shuffle them and put them in a pile, face down.
2 Hold up a card and a child's name and ask him or her a question, as above.

Variant 2
1 Divide the cards into two piles, one for each team. The cards should be face down.
2 Take cards from alternate piles, asking questions, as in the basic game.

Variant 3
1 Give out the cards to the class. Optionally, tell the class to circulate the cards until you shout *Stop!*
2 Ask questions, as in the basic game.

Variant 4
To practise written answers:
1 Divide the class into two teams.
2 Ask a question and tell all the class to write the answer.
3 Choose a child from one team and ask to see his answer.
4 If it is correct, give his team one point. If it is incorrect, choose a child from the other team and look at his. Give him the point if it is correct.
5 Write the correct word or sentence on the board. Tell the class to correct any mistakes they have made.
6 The first team to get (3) points is the winner.

Variant 5

Language	Cards
What's this/that? What are these/those? + the lexis of the cards, e.g.	
1 Teacher: *What's this/that?* Player X: *It's a giraffe.*	1 Sings., Places
2 Teacher: *What's this/that?* Player X: *It's bread.*	2 Uncs.
3 Teacher: *What are these/those?* Player X: *They're giraffes.*	3 Plurals

Numbers The whole class, optionally as a team competition.

Procedure

1 Select a number of cards. Keep half and give half to a volunteer. Stand him at a certain distance.
2 Show the front of a card and ask any child (Player X) *What's this?/What are these?* Player X replies, e.g. *It's a giraffe./They're giraffes.*
3 Tell the volunteer to show a card, point to it, and ask any child *What's that?/What are those?* Player X replies, e.g. *They're giraffes.*
   Individuals can replace the teacher. If this is played as a team competition, let a player consult two friends.
4 The first team to get (5) points is the winner.

Variant 6

Language	Cards
Any true statement suggested by a card, affirmative or negative, e.g.	
1 All tenses of the verb, e.g. simple past: *I played/didn't play football at the weekend.*	1 any set(s) especially Verbs
2 Modal verbs (must, mustn't, should, shouldn't, etc.), e.g. *We mustn't eat in class.*	2 all sets, mixed

Procedure

1 Teach the affirmative and negative of the language item, e.g. the simple past.

2 Hold up a card and ask a child to give you a true sentence. (The sentence must be true, not just correct). For example, the 'play football' card may suggest to the child *I played football at the weekend.*
3 If this is played as a team competition, the first team to get (3) points is the winner.

 24
Funniest story

Description This game encourages children to produce simple narratives.

Language	Cards
1 Narrative (all tenses).	any set(s)
2 Connectors (and, but, then, so, etc.), e.g. *Every Saturday I play tennis. Then I go swimming, and then I go to the zoo to see this elephant.*	

Space Normal classroom.

Numbers The whole class.

Procedure

1 Divide the class into groups of (5) children.
2 Give each group (5) cards from any set or sets.
3 Tell them to prepare a funny story, using the animals, objects, etc. shown on the cards. They can use the cards in any order they like.
4 The groups come to the front of the class, one group at a time, to tell their story. As each child speaks he shows the front of his card. Children who are waiting to speak show the back of the card. E.g.
   Player 1: *Every Saturday I play tennis.* (shows the tennis card)
   Player 2: *Then I go swimming.* (shows the swim card)
   Player 3: *And then I go to the zoo to see this elephant.* (shows the elephant card).
5 The group which tells the funniest story, in the teacher's opinion, is the winner.

25 Giant steps and fairy steps

Description This game is traditional in many countries. Players are instructed to move forwards in a certain way, e.g. ten flea steps.

Language	Materials
Take (ten) (flea) steps.	

Space This game probably requires the whole classroom, or the playground.

Numbers The whole class.

Procedure

1 A volunteer, the 'grandmother', sits on a chair, and the rest of the class stand at some distance from her.

2 The 'grandmother' gives instructions to individual players telling them to move towards her in a certain way, e.g. Grandmother: *Joe, take ten flea steps. Sue, take five ballet dancer steps.*

3 Joe and Sue then move forwards as directed. Define the steps in some way, e.g. flea steps are steps with the toes of the foot touching the heel of the other foot, kangaroo steps are with both feet together, etc.

4 If you think that Joe and Sue have cheated by taking steps which are too large, say *Go back to the beginning!* If necessary, help 'grandmother' by suggesting types of steps.

5 When a player gets near 'grandmother' he touches her. He does not have to touch her immediately; he can wait for a good moment. He then tries to run back to safety (across a line, touching a wall, etc.) before 'grandmother' catches him.

6 If she catches him, he is now the 'grandmother', and the game starts again.

Alternative language

Parts of the body + left/right, e.g.
Touch your left ear and take ten flea steps.

Variant

Language	Materials
Take ten flea steps if you're wearing/carrying something blue.	

Procedure

Play as above, except that the players carry their school bags. 'Grandmother' gives instructions to move forwards, e.g. *Take ten flea steps if you're wearing something blue.* All the players who are wearing something blue move forwards.

 26 Guess

Description Guessing games are simple but popular.

Language	Cards
The lexis of the cards, e.g. Player 1: *What animal is this?* Player X: *It's a giraffe.*	any set(s)

Space Normal classroom.

Numbers The whole class, optionally as a team competition.

Procedure

1 A volunteer (Player 1) stands in front of the class and shows the back of a card. He asks any pupil (X) *What animal is this?*

2 Player X tries to guess. Optionally, tell both players to concentrate and present this as an exercise in telepathy.

3 If this is played as a team competition, Player 1 speaks to a pupil in the other team. The team are allowed three guesses. They get three points if they guess at the first attempt, two at the second attempt, and one at the third attempt. The first team to get (10) points is the winner.

Alternative language

1 The present progressive, e.g.
   Player 1: *What animal am I looking at?*
   Player X: *You're looking at a cat.*/*Are you looking at a cat?*

2 Have got, e.g.
   Player 1: *What animal have I got?*
   Player X: *You've got a cat.*/*Have you got a cat?*

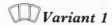 *Variant 1*

Procedure

1 Divide the class into two teams.
2 Select a pupil from each team and stand him in front of the *other* team, holding a card.
3 The teams have alternate guesses, and the first team to guess correctly wins.

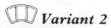 *Variant 2*

Procedure

1 Divide the class into two teams.
2 Send two pupils, one from each team, out of the room.
3 The teams choose an animal, or object. Each team whispers the animal or object to you, so that the other team cannot hear.
4 The two pupils come back, and each stands in front of the other pupil's team.
5 The two pupils have alternate guesses.

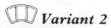 *Variant 3*

Procedure

1 Divide the class into (4) groups, and stand them in different parts of the room.
2 Send one pupil from each group out of the room. These (4) pupils meet outside and choose an animal, object, etc.
3 They come back, and whisper it to you. Then they go to groups which are not their own.
4 The groups try to guess, with one guess per person, in turn.
5 The first group to guess correctly receives all the pupils who went outside.
6 The game ends after (15) minutes, and the group with most members is the winner. If one group has swallowed all the other groups before this time, it is the winner.

27 Hangman

Description This is one of the most popular games in the classroom. Players try to 'hang' a man, as described below.

Language	Materials
1 The alphabet. 2 The written form of words (normally, nouns).	

Space Normal classroom.

Numbers The whole class.

Procedure

1 Divide the class into two teams.
2 Tell each team to choose a word. They can look for it in the course book, if they wish, but the class must have seen it before. They write the word down and show it to you. Check that it is correctly spelt.
3 A volunteer from one team writes a number of dashes on the board, each dash representing a letter of the word, e.g. nurse becomes _____ He should have the written word with him for reference.
4 The other team call out letters of the alphabet, one at a time. They can call out any letter they wish, but it is normal to begin with the vowels, as most words have a vowel.
5 If a letter is in the word, the volunteer writes it in, e.g. _____E
   If it is not in the word, the volunteer can begin to 'hang the man'. He does this by drawing the first line of the following picture. As other wrong guesses are made, he adds other lines. The lines are numbered in the drawing below to show the order in which they should be drawn.

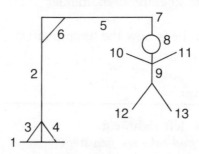

6 If the volunteer hangs the man, his team wins. If the other team guesses the word first, it wins.

Obviously, the drawing need not be of a hanged man; some teachers may prefer a drawing of their own.

28 Happy families

Description This is a classic children's game. Players try to be the first to put down all their cards, in pairs. A pair is composed of two animal cards, two object cards or two person cards.

Language	Cards
Requests with 'Can I have?' Pronoun 'one', e.g. Player 1: *Can I have an object, please?* Player X: *Yes, here you are.* or *Sorry, I haven't got one.*	all sets, mixed

Space Normal classroom.

Numbers Groups of 3 or 4 players (4 is a good number), with 3+ cards each.

Procedure

1 The leader shuffles the cards and deals them.
2 Players look at their cards and put any pairs they have down on the table.
3 Player 1 asks any other player (X) for a card of a certain type, animal, object, or person, in order to make a pair, e.g. *Can I have an object, please?* Players must already have one card of that type before they can ask for another one. If Player X has an object card, she must give it to Player 1, saying *Yes, here you are.* Player 1 then puts down the pair and asks again until somebody refuses him a card. It is then the turn of the player who refused him. If Player X does not have an object card she says *Sorry, I haven't got one*, and it is then her turn to ask any other player for a card.
4 The first player to put down all his cards in pairs is the winner.

Alternative language

Requests with 'Have you got a(n)?' e.g.
Player 1: *Have you got an object?*
Player X: *Yes, here you are.* or *Sorry, I haven't.*

Variant 1

If there are enough cards available, the following variant is recommended:

1 Put extra cards in a pool (a pile, face down in the middle).
2 When players have made all the pairs they can, they pick up cards from the pool, first saying the type of card they want, e.g. *Object.*
3 If they get the card they want, they put the pair down and have another turn.
4 If they pick up a card which they did not want, they must put it on the bottom of the pile, and it is then the turn of the player sitting next to them.
5 As before, the first player to put down all his cards in pairs is the winner.

Variant 2

Language	Cards
Requests with 'Can we have some (more)?' e.g. Player 1: *Can we have some (more) chocolate/sweets, please?* Player X: *Yes, here you are.* or *Sorry, we haven't got any chocolate/sweets.*	Uncs. and/ or Plurals

Procedure

1 Take 18 cards (the Uncountables set, or the Plurals set, or a mixture of the two sets).
2 Divide the class into two teams, and appoint a leader for each team.
3 Give the leaders three cards each, making sure that all six cards show different animals or objects.
4 Stand three volunteers around the room. Give them the remaining cards, four cards each. If there is a Joker among these cards, tell the player who has it to hold it but ignore it.
5 The leaders of the teams ask the volunteers for the cards they need to make pairs, e.g. *Can we have some more chocolate, please?* In this variant, pairs are made of two cards showing the same item, e.g. the two chocolate cards. The leaders can consult their teams.

6 The first team to collect all three pairs is the winner.

Alternative language

Requests with 'Have you got any?' e.g.
Player 1: *Have you got any chocolate/sweets?*
Player X: *Yes, here you are.* or
No (, I haven't.) (Sorry.)

 # 29 Hat game

Player 4
Player 3
Player 2
Player 1
Player 1
Teacher

Description This is a new game. It is a kind of relay race in which players have to answer a question correctly before they are allowed to run. The first line of players to finish is the winner.

Language	Cards/Materials
Present progressive, e.g. Player 1: *What am I doing?* Player 2: *You're swimming.*	2 hats □□ Verbs

Space An open area in the classroom. If played outdoors, distances can be greater, e.g. to a tree or wall and back.

Numbers Two teams, with (5) pupils representing each team.

Procedure

1 Divide the class into two teams, and choose (5) players from each team.

2 Stand the players in two lines, facing you, as shown in the illustration. The players at the back of each line stand on a chair, holding 4+ cards from the Verbs set.

3 Put three chairs behind you, and put hats on the two nearest chairs.

4 Say *Ready! Steady! Go!* The two players at the front of each line (Player 1 in the illustration) run to the nearest chair, pick up the hat and put it on. They then run around the three chairs, and back to their places.

5 The player at the back of each line then holds up the first Verb card and Player 1 must look at it and mime what he sees – in this example it is the 'swim' card.

6 Player 1 asks *What am I doing?* and Player 2 guesses, e.g. *You're swimming.*

7 If the answer is correct, say *O.K.!* Player 1 then gives the hat to Player 2 and goes back to his seat.

8 Player 2 puts the hat on, runs around the 3 chairs, comes back to her place, and mimes the next picture, which the child on the chair is now holding up. Player 3 must guess what she is doing.

9 If a pupil cannot answer the question *What am I doing?* in (5) seconds, say *Go to the back!* and the pupil must go to the back of the line.

10 The first team to finish wins. A team finishes when all (4) players have run around the chairs.

Alternative language	Cards/Materials
1 Imperatives, e.g. Player 1: *Jump!* (Player 2 then jumps)	2 hats □□ **1** Verbs
2 Be + noun, e.g. Player 1: *What am I?* Player 2: *You're a nurse.*	□□ **2** Profs.

Variant 1

Language	Cards/Materials
The lexis of the cards, e.g. **1** Player 2: *What's that?* Player 1: *It's a giraffe.* **2** Player 2: *What are they?* Player 1: *They're horses.*	2 hats **1** Sings., Places, Uncs. **2** Plurals

Procedure

This is played in the same way as the basic game, except that Player 2 points at the card and asks the question.

Variant 2

Language	Cards/Materials
Present progressive, e.g. Player 1: *Bye-bye!/Goodbye.* Player 2: *Where are you going?* Player 1: *I'm going to the cinema.*	2 hats Places

Procedure

1 Arrange the lines of players as in the basic game. (The three chairs behind the teacher are not necessary.)
2 Give Player 1 in each line a hat. Tell them to put the hats on.
3 Player 1 says *Bye-bye!* and Player 2 asks *Where are you going?* Player 1 replies *I'm going to the cinema.*
4 Player 1 runs in a circle around the outside of the two chairs at the back of the lines, and back.
5 He gives Player 2 the hat and returns to his seat.
6 It is then Player 2's turn to say *Bye-bye!* to Player 3, and so on.
7 The first team to finish wins. A team finishes when all (4) players have run around the chairs.

Variant 3

Language	Cards/Materials
Present perfect, e.g. Player 1: *Bye-bye!* Player 2: *Bye-bye!/Goodbye.* *Where have you been?* Player 1: *I've been to the cinema.*	2 hats Places

Procedure

1 Arrange the lines of players as in the basic game. (The three chairs behind the teacher are not necessary.)
2 Give Player 1 in each line a hat. Tell them to put them on.
3 Player 1 says *Bye-bye!* and Player 2 replies *Bye-bye!*
4 Player 1 then runs in a circle around the outside of the two chairs at the back of the lines, and comes back.
5 Player 2 asks *Where have you been?* and Player 1 replies *I've been to the cinema.*
6 Player 1 gives Player 2 the hat and goes back to his seat. It is then Player 2's turn to say *Bye-bye!* to Player 3, and so on.
7 The first team to finish wins. A team finishes when all the players have run around the chairs and answered the question *Where have you been?*

 30 House

Description This is a new game with a mixture of skill (memory) and luck (the dice). Cards are arranged face down in the form of a house; players try to predict whether cards are animal, object or person cards, and if they predict correctly they are allowed to take the cards and start to build another house with them.

Language	Cards/Materials
The rooms of a house, e.g. *That animal's in the bathroom.*	9 cards: a mixture of animal, object and person cards 1 dice per group something to attach the cards to the board 1 marker per group: a small piece of paper with the name of the group leader, to mark the place of each group

Space Normal classroom.

Numbers The whole class, with 3 or 4 groups playing against each other.

Procedure

1 Divide the class into three or four groups. Appoint a leader in each group, and give him a dice. For each group, prepare a piece of paper with the name of the leader, to mark his place, e.g. JOE

2 Put the cards on the board in the shape of a house. Put the house on one half of the board, to leave room for another house on the other half. Label the rooms as shown:

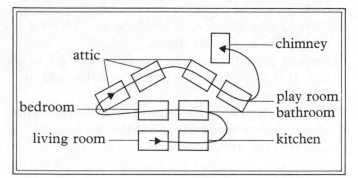

3 The leader of the first group throws a dice. He then moves his marker forwards the number thrown, following the route marked by the arrow. If he throws a 3, for example, he lands on the bathroom.

4 He then tries to predict the type of card he has landed on (animal, object, or person) and says, for example, *That animal's in the bathroom*. He turns the card over, and if he is right, (that is, if the card does show an animal) he takes the card and starts to build a new house with it, putting it in the same position as in the original house:

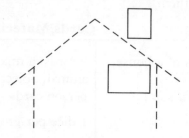

The same group then carries on until it fails to predict a card, and then it is the turn of the next group. The card is left face down.

5 When players throw their dice, the number thrown refers to the cards still left in the house. They jump over any missing cards. For example, if the bathroom card is missing, the bedroom becomes number 3.

6 When groups have been around all the house they go directly back to the beginning, and start again, in a kind of circle, without stopping at the chimney (unless they land on it).

7 The winner is the player who puts the last card in the new house.

Alternative language

There's, e.g.
There 's an animal in the bathroom.

Variant 1

Language	Cards
Present progressive, Who? and Where? e.g. **1** Player X: *He's swimming in the bathroom.* **2** Teacher: *Who (is)? Where's he swimming?*	Verbs

Procedure

Play as above, but with the set of verbs. Since pupils tend to remember only the verb, and say e.g. *swimming*, the teacher can ask, e.g.: *Who is?* and *where's he swimming?*

Variant 2

Language	Cards/Materials
Is/are there? + the lexis of the cards, e.g. **1** *Is there a giraffe* **2** *Is there any bread* *in the bathroom?* **3** *Are there any giraffes*	1 dice per group **1** Sings., Profs. **2** Uncs. **3** Plurals

Procedure

Play with the whole class, as described in Dice games on p. 6–7 of the Introduction. Put the cards on the board, showing the front of the card, for 30 seconds. Tell the class to try to memorize them. Then turn the cards round, to show the back. When a player lands on a card he asks, e.g. *Is there a giraffe in the bathroom?* The teacher, or a volunteer, turns the card round and says *Yes (, there is).*, or *No (, there isn't)*. Plural cards will of course require *Are there?*

31 I can swim

Description This is a team competition involving mime. Players get points for showing that they understand a question, e.g. Can you swim?

Language	Cards
Can (ability), e.g. Player 1: *I can swim. Can you swim?* Player X: *Yes (, I can). or No (, I can't).*	Verbs

Space Normal classroom.

Numbers The whole class, as a team competition.

Procedure

1 Shuffle the set of Verbs and divide it into two equal piles.
2 Put the piles face down on the table, one for each team.
3 Individuals from each team take it in turns to come to the front of the class. They look at the top card, without letting anybody else see it. In the example below, Player 1 has picked up the 'swim' card; he and Player X are in the same team. They both tell the truth. Player 1 speaks, and Player X speaks and mimes.
   Player 1: *I can/can't swim. Can you swim?*
   Player X: *Yes, I can./No, I can't.*
   Player X then mimes swimming; if she says she can't swim, she mimes swimming badly.
4 Give a maximum of two points: one to Player 1 for his two sentences (I can swim. Can you swim?), and one to Player X for replying and miming.
5 It is then the turn of somebody from the other team to come to the front, pick up a card, and say, e.g. *I can jump. Can you jump?*
6 The game ends when all the cards have been picked up, and the team with most points wins.

32 I claim

Description This is a game from a mother-tongue collection. Players name as many classroom objects as possible beginning with a given letter of the alphabet.

Language	Materials
1 The lexis of classroom objects. 2 The alphabet.	

Space Normal classroom.

Numbers The whole class, as a team competition.

Procedure

1 Divide the class into (2) teams. Appoint a scorer for each team.
2 Any player can claim a letter of the alphabet if he can name an object or objects beginning with that letter, e.g. Teacher: *B.* Player X: *I claim B: blackboard.*
3 If any other player (Player Y) can see another object beginning with the letter, he puts his hand up and says *I claim B: blackboard and book.*
4 If no other player claims the letter after (10) seconds, Player Y wins it for his team.
5 The winning team is the first team to win (3) letters. Alternatively, set a time limit, e.g. 10 minutes, and the team which wins the most letters in that time is the winner.

33 I spy

Desciption This is one of the best known children's games. Players try to guess an object beginning with a certain letter.

Language	Materials
1 *I spy with my little eye something beginning with D.* 2 The lexis of classroom objects.	

Space Normal classroom.

Numbers The whole class.

Procedure

1 A child says *I spy with my little eye something beginning with (D).* (He can say any letter he wishes).
2 Individual children try to guess the object, e.g. *Door.*
3 The child who guesses successfully then says *I spy with my little eye something beginning with (P).*, and the rest of the class try to guess.

4 The game ends whenever you wish.

Alternative language

> **1** Other lexis, e.g.
> *I'm thinking of something in the kitchen beginning with D.*
>
> **2** Other tenses of the verb, e.g.
> *I went to the kitchen yesterday and saw something beginning with D.*

34
Jumping the line

Description This game is sometimes found in mother-tongue collections. The leader makes a statement and players jump to the TRUE or FALSE side of a line drawn on the floor.

Language	Cards/Materials
The lexis of the cards: **1** Singular nouns, e.g. (a) giraffe **2** Uncountable nouns, e.g. bread **3** Plural nouns, e.g. giraffes	a piece of chalk **1** Sings., Profs., Places **2** Uncs. **3** Plurals

Space An open area in the classroom, or the playground.

Numbers The whole class. If there is not enough room for everyone to play, divide the class into two teams as described in Variant 2 below.

Procedure

1 Draw a line on the floor and mark one side TRUE and the other FALSE. If necessary, for reasons of space, more than one line can be drawn, in different parts of the room.

2 Hold up a card and say, e.g. *A giraffe.*

3 If this is true, the players jump to the TRUE side of the line (unless they are there already). They must jump with their feet together. If it is not true, players jump to the FALSE side (unless they are

there already).

4 Players who make a mistake are out, or lose one of their three 'lives'. The game ends when all the players except one are out.

Alternative language

> Any true or false statements, e.g.
> Teacher: *Joe's wearing a red pullover.*

Variant 1
Procedure

1 Play as described in the basic game, except that you will need one chalk line for each team. If space is a problem, choose (5) representatives of each team; the representatives go back to their seats when they are out, and are replaced by other members of the team.

2 Each time a player is out, this counts as a point against his team.

3 The team with the least points against it after 10 minutes is the winner.

Variant 2

Language	Materials
Any two lexical sets, e.g. Animal and Object, Food and Not Food, Day and Month, Colour and Number, Clothes and Parts of the body.	a piece of chalk

Procedure

1 Replace the words TRUE and FALSE in the basic game by one of the above pairs, e.g. ANIMAL and OBJECT.

2 Call out an animal or an object, e.g. *Giraffe.*

3 The players jump – in this example – to the ANIMAL side.

Variant 3

Language	Cards
This/that/these/those + the lexis of the cards, e.g. **1** *This is/That's a giraffe.* **2** *This is/That's bread.* **3** *These/Those are giraffes.*	**1** Sings., Places **2** Uncs. **3** Plurals

Procedure

1 Select a number of cards. Keep half, and give half to a volunteer, who stands at a certain distance.
2 Hold up a card and make a statement about it, using 'this' or 'these', e.g. *This is a giraffe.* Mix true and false statements.
3 Tell the volunteer to hold up a card. Make a true or false statement about it, using 'that' or 'those', e.g. *That's a giraffe.*

Variant 4

Language	Cards

What's this/that/these/those? + the lexis of the cards, e.g.
 	
1 Teacher: *What's this/that?*
   Player X: *It's a giraffe.*
 	
2 Teacher: *What's this/that?*
   Player X: *It's bread.*
 	
3 Teacher: *What are these/those?*
   Player X: *They're giraffes.*
	1 Sings., Places
	
	2 Uncs.
	
	3 Plurals

Procedure

Play in the same way as Variant 3 above, with a volunteer holding cards at a distance. Ask any pupil in the class (Player X) a question about a card, e.g. *What's this?* Tell him he can make a true or a false statement, e.g. *It's a giraffe.* The class respond to his statement by jumping or not jumping.

35 Kim's game

Description This memory game was described by Rudyard Kipling in his book *Kim*. Players have a limited time in which to try to memorize a number of objects. The game is described below for use with cards, but it can of course be done with real objects, as in the original.

Language	Cards
The lexis of the cards (spoken and written).	any set(s)

Space Normal classroom.

Numbers The whole class, as a team competition.

Procedure

1 Show (10) cards to the class, each one for (3) seconds. Tell the class to try to memorize them.
2 The class write down what they can remember, working in pairs.
3 Ask which pair in each team has got the most words, and take their lists.
4 Starting with one list, write one word at a time on the board, exactly as they have written it.
5 Give one point if the word is correct. If it is not correct, give the team (10) seconds to correct it. If they correct it, give them one point, and if not, give them half a point. Always leave the word on the board correctly spelt so that the class do not learn the wrong form.
6 Work through both lists in this way.
7 The team with most points is the winner.

36 Kim's game around the room

Description This is a memory game similar to Kim's Game.

Language	Cards
The lexis of the cards + prepositions of place, e.g. Teacher: *Where's the giraffe?* Player X: *It's over there/next to the door/on the table.*	any set(s)

Space Normal classroom.

Numbers The whole class, as a team competition.

Procedure

1 Walk around the room leaving (11) cards at different points. Show the front of each card for (3) seconds, and then turn it round to show the back. Tell the class to try to remember the cards. Keep a list of the cards used.

2 Select a pupil from one team and ask where the animals or objects are, referring to the list if necessary, e.g.
Teacher: *Where's the giraffe?*
Player X: *It's over there/next to the door.*
Other useful language:
Teacher: *Which one? This one?*
Joe: *No, the next one/the one to the left.*

3 Turn the card round. If Player X is right, she keeps the card. If she is wrong, put it back where it was.

4 Do the same with a pupil from the other team, and so on.

5 The team that wins most cards is the winner.

*Variant*

Language	Cards
Narrative (any tense) and connectors (when, and, but, etc.), e.g. Teacher: *I went to the zoo yesterday. I was looking at an elephant when I heard a strange noise. It was a lion . . .*	any set(s)

Procedure

1 Place (11) cards around the room, as described in the basic game. Keep a record of the cards used.

2 Tell a 'story' which contains the animals, objects, etc. on the cards. The 'story' can be a simple narrative suggested by the cards.

3 When pupils hear the name of an animal, object, etc. that is on one of the cards, they put their hands up.

4 Select pupils from alternate teams to go and turn a card round.

5 If it is the right card, they keep it, and the team with most cards at the ends wins.

6 Optionally, pupils can replace the teacher and tell their own story, with different cards.

37 Kim's game with dice

Description As the title indicates, this is a variation on Kim's Game. It involves some luck (the dice) and some skill (memory). Players win cards by landing on them, and remembering which animal, object, etc. is on the cards.

Language	Cards/Materials
The lexis of the cards, e.g. **1** (a) giraffe **2** bread **3** giraffes	1 + dice per group ![cards] **1** Sings., Profs., Places ![cards] **2** Uncs. ![cards] **3** Plurals

Space Normal classroom.

Numbers Groups of (4) players, with 3 cards each.

Procedure

1 The leader shuffles the cards, and places them face down on the table, in any pattern he wishes, e.g. a straight line, or a circle.

2 He turns the cards up for (30 seconds) and then turns them face down again.

3 The players decide which is the first card, and in which direction they are going to move.

4 Player 1 throws the dice and, touching the corresponding card, guesses what it is, e.g. *A giraffe*. In the illustration he has thrown a 3:

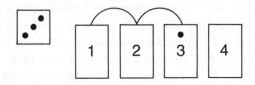

5 He turns the third card face up. If the card does in fact show a giraffe, he wins it, and takes it. If it is not a giraffe, it is left face down in the same position.

6 It is then the turn of Player 2 who counts from one upwards, ignoring any missing cards. That is to say, if the third card has been won the next card becomes number 3, as shown:

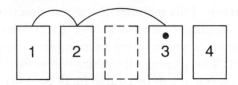

7 The winner is the player who wins most cards.

Alternative language

Animal, object, person.

34

As an alternative play as in the basic game, but players do not name the animal or object. Instead they say *Animal, Object* or *Person*.

Variant 1

All the cards are numbered at the beginning. They keep the same numbers throughout the game and if a player lands on a missing card, he cannot win it, and must wait for his next turn:

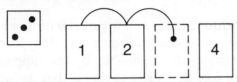

A player can throw either one or two dice, but he must first say how many dice he is going to throw. If he does not say this, he can only throw one.

Variant 2

Language	Cards/Materials
There is/are + the lexis of the cards, e.g.	Blu-tack to fix cards to blackboard 1 dice per group
1 *There's a giraffe* **2** *There's some bread* ⎱ *in that picture.* **3** *There are some giraffes*	1 Sings., Profs., Places 2 Uncs. 3 Plurals

Procedure

Play with the whole class, as described in Dice games, p. 6–7 of the Introduction.

Variant 3

Language	Cards/Materials
A lot of, not much, not many + the lexis of the cards, e.g.	Blu-tack to fix cards blackboard 1 dice per group
1 *There's a lot of bread* *There isn't much bread* ⎱ *in that picture.*	1 Uncs.
2 *There are a lot of giraffes* *There aren't many giraffes* ⎱ *in that picture.*	2 Plurals

Procedure

Play with the whole class, as described in Dice games, p. 6–7 of the Introduction.

38 Left, right and centre

Description This is an English mother-tongue game. Players try to be the one to put the last card in the centre.

Language	Cards/Materials
Requests, e.g. Player X: *Can I have a card, please?* Player 1: *Yes, here you are.*	1 dice per group any set(s)

Space Normal classroom.

Numbers Groups can be of any size, but the game goes well in groups of 3, with 3 cards per player.

Procedure

1 Put the following on the board for reference:

> 1 – Left
> 2 – Right
> 3, 4 – Centre
> 5, 6 – Keep it.

2 The leader of each group gives out the cards, three per player. The players can look at them. In fact, the cards are simply used as objects in this game, and could be replaced by coins, buttons, etc.

3 Player 1 throws the dice. Refer to the board: if he throws a 1 he gives a card to the player on his left, if he throws a 2 he gives a card to the player on his right, if he throws a 3 or a 4 he puts a card in the centre, and if he throws a 5 or 6 he keeps the card.

If Player 1 throws a 1 or a 2, the player who is going to receive a card must ask for it: if he forgets to ask for it, Player 1 is not obliged to give it to him.

4 Player 1 passes the dice to Player 2, and so on. A player can only throw the dice if he has a card. If he does not have a card, he misses his turn – but

he is not out of the game, because somebody will probably give him a card.

5 The winner is the player who puts the last card in the centre.

Variant

Language	Cards/Materials
Offers, e.g. Player 1: *Would you like/Do you want a card?* Player X: *Yes, please . . . .* *Thank you.*	1 dice per group any set(s)

Play as described in the basic game, except that: if Player 1 throws a 1 or a 2, he must offer a card to Player X, instead of Player X having to ask for it. If a player forgets to say *Would you like/Do you want a card?* he must then give the other player a second card, if he has one to give him.

39 Map game

Description This is a simple team competition. Players win points by naming countries and indicating them on a map.

Language	Materials
1 Countries and languages. **2** Simple present, e.g. Teacher: *Where do they speak Spanish?*	a map of the world

Space Normal classroom.

Numbers The whole class, as a team competition.

Procedure

1 Put up a map of the world.

2 Divide the class into (2) teams. Ask for a volunteer from the first team (Player X, below):
Teacher: *Where do they speak Spanish?*
Player X: *In Spain.*
Teacher: *Where's Spain?*
Player X: *Here.* (Points to Spain on the map).

3 Give a maximum of two points: one for knowing the country and another for knowing where it is.

4 Ask for a volunteer from the other team, and so on.

5 The first team to get (10) points is the winner.

40 Memory

Description This is a new game, with some luck (guessing) and some skill (memory). Players try to win as many cards as possible, by touching cards which are face down and saying if they are animal, object or person cards.

Language	Cards
Animal, object, person.	all sets, mixed

Space Normal classroom.

Numbers Groups of 3 or 4 players, with 3 cards each. It goes well with 3 players.

Procedure

1 Put the following on the board for reference. It shows the order in which cards must be won.

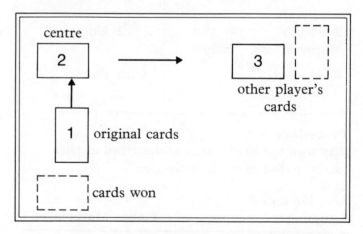

2 The leader shuffles the cards and deals them face down, so that each player has a pile of cards in front of him, (the 'original cards' in the illustration above). Players cannot look at the cards. Explain that these cards do not yet belong to anybody: players have to win them.

3 The first player tries to predict the top card of his pile, and says, e.g. *Animal.* He then turns it over. If it is an animal, he keeps it and starts a second pile, horizontally, of cards won. He then carries on trying to predict cards until he makes a mistake. If he guesses wrongly, he puts the card in the centre, face down. It is then the turn of

Player 2, and so on, around the group. The game normally looks something like this:

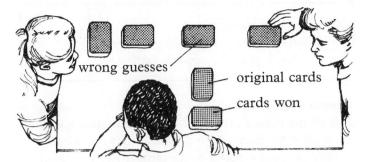

wrong guesses

original cards

cards won

4 Refer to the board. A player who guesses a card correctly carries on, and if he wins all the cards in his original pile he then moves on to cards in the centre (if there are any) and tries to win those. If he wins those he tries to win the other players' original cards, in rotation. He cannot win cards from the other players' horizontal piles of cards which they have won.

5 The game ends when all the cards have been won, that is, when all the cards are in the horizontal piles. The player with most cards is the winner.

Variant

This variant is for 2 players only, as it is too difficult with more. Play as described above, except that after winning Player 2's original cards, Player 1 moves on to the horizontal pile of cards won by Player 2. The winner is the player who wins all the cards. This variant has amusing changes of fortune by which the player who has almost won is not necessarily the winner. Both players have a chance of winning right up to the final card.

41 Mime

Description Mime is not exactly a game, perhaps, but children probably consider that it is: they do it at parties and in their spontaneous play in the playground. It is a useful classroom activity, because it produces a lot of language. Mime can easily be combined with the 'revision games': see the section on revision games on p. 8 of the Introduction.

Language	Materials
any lexis	

Space Normal classroom.
Numbers The whole class.
Procedure

1 Invite a volunteer to come to the front of the class.

2 Tell him to mime something or somebody, e.g. *Mime an animal/an object/a profession.* Volunteers can mime an object, e.g. a watch, by pretending to use it, or by pretending to be it, e.g. by holding their arms like the hands of a watch.

3 When the other children think they recognise the object, animal, etc., they put their hands up. The child who identifies the mime correctly replaces the volunteer.

Variant 1

Language	Materials
Any sentences, e.g. *I'm a policeman.* *I saw a policeman yesterday.*	

Procedure

1 Put a model sentence on the board showing the part of the sentence that does not change, in this example: I'm _____

2 Demonstrate by miming a sentence, e.g. *I'm a policeman.* It is not necessary to mime every word: short words like 'a', 'the' and 'of' will be added later. Begin by pointing to yourself to elicit *I'm.* Children who think they know what you mean put their hands up. If somebody says *You* or *You're,* point to the model on the board. Then mime 'policeman'.

3 A volunteer replaces you, and mimes a sentence of his own. If the sentence includes the word *I* or *You,* as in the present example, the person who has just mimed should repeat it before sitting down: *Yes, I'm a policeman.*

4 A few basic gestures are needed when miming. Some encouraging hand signal meaning 'Yes, keep guessing' is useful when the class are in the right area. Another useful signal is 'more or less'. Some countries have a hand signal for this; facial expressions can also suggest it. With longer sentences, it may be necessary to go back to the beginning and start again. Some signal meaning 'Stop' will convey this. If the sentence contains an expression of time, e.g. 'yesterday', one can signal earlier or later by pointing to one's watch and indicating a forwards or backwards rotation of the hands.

In the illustration below, the volunteer mimes *I play tennis every day.*, in four steps. 1) He points to himself to elicit 'I'. 2) He mimes 'play tennis'. 3) He points to the model to elicit 'every'. 4) He waits for somebody to say 'Sunday'. The teacher will then say *Do it again.*, and he will repeat the four steps with the whole class shouting out the words. Finally, to avoid possible confusion with the meaning *I* and *You*, the teacher will tell him to say *Yes, I play tennis every Sunday.*

I —————— every ———————

If the class have difficulty with any word, e.g. Sunday, the teacher can help, e.g. by pretending to be in church.

Variant 2
Language

	Materials
Any written sentences.	

Procedure
As above, but:
1 Ask the class to write a sentence.
2 When volunteers come to do their mime, tell them to bring the sentence with them. Correct any mistakes in it.
3 When the class have guessed the mime, the volunteer reads out his sentence.

Variant 3
Language

	Materials
Any true sentences, e.g. *I am going (to go) to the cinema tomorrow.* *I went/didn't go to the cinema yesterday.*	

Procedure
1 Tell the class to think of a true sentence, e.g. about what they really did yesterday, or what they are really going to do tomorrow.
2 Ask a volunteer to whisper his sentence to you first, and then mime it. The class try to guess it.

Variant 4
Language

	Cards
Any sentences containing the lexis of a card, e.g.	any set(s), e.g.
1 *I'm an elephant.*	1 Sings.
2 *I'm swimming.*	2 Verbs.

1 Put a model sentence on the board e.g. I'm ———.
2 Divide the class into (2) teams and appoint a scorer in each.
3 Take a set of cards, shuffle them and put them in a pile face down.
4 Offer the top card to a volunteer from the first team. Tell him to put what he sees in a sentence and mime it. Refer to the model on the board.
5 The volunteer stands in front of his own team and mimes the sentence, e.g. *I'm a policeman.*
6 Children in the volunteer's team put their hands up if they think they know the complete sentence.
7 Give the team three attempts to say the sentence. Give three points if they say it at the first attempt, two points at the second attempt, and one at the third.
8 It is then the turn of the other team, and so on.
9 The team that gets most points is the winner.

Variant 5
Language

	Materials
The imperative (e.g. read) and, optionally, any sentence containing the verb (e.g. I'm reading).	

Procedure

1 Divide the class into two teams and appoint a scorer in each.

2 Whisper the imperative, e.g. read, into a volunteer's ear.

3 If he mimes correctly, give a point to his team.

4 Optionally, the volunteer then asks any child in his own team *What am I doing?* If the child replies correctly, e.g. *You're reading.*, give the team another point.

5 Ask for a volunteer from the other team, and so on.

6 The first team to get (6) points is the winner.

Variant 6

Language	Materials
The imperative (e.g. read) and, optionally, any sentence containing the verb (e.g. I'm reading).	Make word cards showing the written imperative of the verbs you want to practise.

Procedure

1 Divide the class into two teams and appoint a scorer in each.

2 Shuffle the word cards and put them in a pile face down.

3 Invite volunteers from alternate teams to come to the front and pick up a card.

4 The volunteers mime what they see, e.g. read.

5 Give them one point if they mime correctly.

6 Optionally, a volunteer can ask any child in his own team *What am I doing?* If the child replies correctly, e.g. *You're reading.*, give the team another point.

7 The first team to get (6) points is the winner.

42 Mine!

Description This is a new memory game. Players try to win as many cards as possible, by remembering who the cards belong to.

Language	Cards
Possessives: Player 1: *This is my card/mine!* or *This is your card/yours!*	any set(s)

Space Normal classroom.

Numbers Groups of 3 or 4 players, with 3 cards each.

Procedure

1 The leader of the group shuffles the cards and then deals three cards face down to each player. Players can look at their cards.

2 Players take it in turns to hold up their cards, showing the front of the cards for five seconds. The other players try to memorize the cards, and who is holding them.

3 All the cards are then collected, shuffled and placed face down on the table, spread out.

4 Player 1 picks up any card and looks at it. If it is his own, he says *This is mine!* If he is right, he wins the card. When a player wins one of his own cards in this way, that card counts as two cards. If Player 1 picks up a card belonging to another player, he says to that player *This is yours!* If he is right, he wins the card.

5 Player 1 carries on winning cards until he makes a mistake. It is then the turn of Player 2, and so on, around the group.

6 The game ends when there are no more cards to be won. The player who has won most cards is the winner.

43 Moors and Christians

Description This is a traditional Spanish game. (Some teachers may prefer to give it a different title.) Players try to run back to their own territory without being touched.

Language	Cards/Materials
1 Numbers: 1 to (20). **2** Any answers to questions put by the teacher. This includes, for example: **a** General revision of past lessons, e.g. Teacher: *How old are you? What's the time?* etc. **b** Tenses of the verb	a piece of chalk optional: any set(s)

Space An open area in the classroom, or the playground.

Numbers The whole class in 2 teams, or (5) representatives of each team.

Procedure

1 Name the teams 'Moors' and 'Christians', or names of your choice.

2 Stand the teams facing each other and number the players from 1 upwards. Keep both teams behind chalk lines drawn on the floor.

3 In the centre draw a rectangle, to represent the prison.

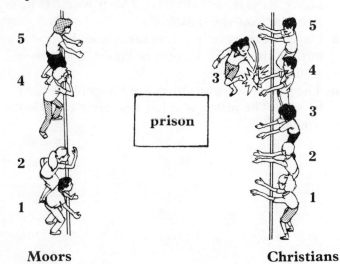

Moors   **Christians**

4 Call out a team and a number, e.g. *Moors, 3!*

5 Player number 3 in the Moors team walks across to the other team, who all hold their hands out in front of them. Beginning at player number 1, he walks down the line stroking the palms of the players in that team. At any moment he can hit a player's palm, hard!

6 As soon as he has done this, he is in danger, and must run back to the safety of his own territory, behind his line. The player he has just hit (Christian 4 in the illustration) can chase him. If Moor 3 gets back home safely, then Christian 4

goes to prison. If Moor 3 is touched before he reaches safety he goes to prison. He can get out of prison:

a if he answers a question put by the teacher, e.g. *How old are you?* (Optionally, the questions can refer to cards, e.g. *What's he doing?*)

b if he is touched by a player from his team who is running back to safety. Prisoners must stay inside the prison until released, but can stretch their hands out to make it easier for the fugitive to touch them.

When there are two or more prisoners from the same team they hold hands, and when one of them is touched, they are all released. But they are not safe until they cross their own line. This means that the pursuer can touch them again, if he can, and send them back to prison.

7 The team with the least prisoners after (10) minutes wins.

44 Mother Magee is coming to stay

Description This is a mother-tongue game. Players try to make each other smile by making funny faces.

Language	Materials
Player 1: *Mother Magee is coming to stay.* Player 2: *What's she like?* Player 1: *She's got (a mouth) like this.*	

Space Normal classroom.

Numbers (4) volunteers in front of the class.

Procedure

1 Stand (4) volunteers in front of the class.

2 The first volunteer (Player 1) says *Mother Magee is coming to stay.*

3 The second (Player 2) asks *What's she like?*

4 The first replies, e.g. *She's got a mouth like this.*, and twists his mouth in an amusing way.

5 Player 2 then turns to Player 3 and repeats the dialogue, but adding a phrase of her own at the end, e.g. *She's got a mouth like this and a nose like this.* She twists her mouth and her nose.

6 It is then the turn of the next volunteer to add another phrase and gesture.

7 Volunteers who smile are out, and are replaced by new volunteers.

8 The game ends whenever the teacher wishes.

45 My father likes apples

Description This game is played in the mother tongue both inside and outside the classroom. Players go through the alphabet, thinking of nouns that begin with the letters, e.g. **a**pples, **b**ooks, **c**ats, etc.

Language	Materials
1 *My father likes apples/books/cats,* etc. **2** The alphabet.	

Space Normal classroom.

Numbers The whole class, as a team competition.

Procedure

1 Divide the class into 2 teams.

2 Tell the first player to think of something beginning with A, and to say that his father likes it, e.g. *My father likes apples.*

3 Tell the second player, who is in the other team, to think of something beginning with B and say, e.g. *My father likes books.*

4 Alternate between the two teams, moving through the alphabet. Give players (10) seconds to think of a word, and let them consult their teams. Give one point for each sentence. There are difficult letters, especially j, q, u, v, x, and z. These can be omitted, or suggestions can be made for future occasions when the game is played.

5 The team with most points at the end of the alphabet (or after 10 minutes) is the winner.

46 My name's Joe

Description This is a simple team competition in which players get one point for each sentence. If the game is played regularly the class soon become fluent in talking about themselves.

Language	Materials
Personal description, e.g. *My name's Joe. My surname's Smith. I'm 9 (years old). I live in Barcelona. I've got two brothers and one sister. My favourite sport is football.*	No materials are needed, but if the class have not played before they may be happier with a cardboard mask in front of their faces.

Space Normal classroom.

Numbers The whole class, as a team competition.

Procedure

1 Divide the class into two teams.

2 Ask a volunteer from the first team to come to the front of the class.

3 Tell him to describe himself. Explain that you will give him one point for each sentence. Give one or two examples in the mother tongue: *My name's Jordi.*, *I'm nine.*, etc. If he is more than ten seconds without beginning a new sentence, say *Stop!* It is then the turn of a volunteer from the other team.

4 When (3) volunteers from each team have described themselves, the team with most points is the winner.

47 Noughts and crosses on the board

Description The game of 'Noughts and crosses', which is normally played by two players, sometimes appears in this form as an adult television competition. Players try to put three noughts or three crosses in a straight line.

Language | **Materials**

1 Numbers 1 to 9.

2 Any answers to questions put by the teacher. This includes, for example:
  a Revision of past lessons, e.g. Teacher: *How old are you? What's the time?*
  b All tenses of the verb.

Space Normal classroom.

Numbers The whole class, as a team competition.

Procedure

1 Put the following on the board.

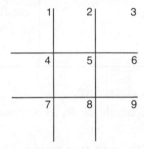

2 Divide the class into two teams and appoint a leader and scorer in each team. One team is Noughts (0) and the other Crosses (X).

3 Ask the leader of the first team (Leader 1) which square he wants, e.g.
  Teacher: *Which square do you want?*
  Leader 1: *Number 5.*
  It is usual to begin by asking for square number 5, as it is the strongest square. If you wish, ask a difficult question for this square.

4 Ask Leader 1 a question, e.g. *How old are you?* He can consult his team. Set a time limit, e.g. 10 seconds. If the answer is correct the scorer writes the symbol of the team in square number 5.

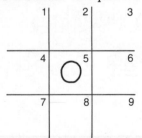

It is then the turn of the other team. If the answer is wrong offer the question to the other team. If they answer correctly, their scorer puts their symbol in the square. If neither team can answer, answer yourself and pass on to the next question.

5 Put questions to alternate teams. The teams try to get three noughts or crosses in a straight line – horizontally, vertically or diagonally. (At times, a team may have to use its symbol to prevent the other team from completing a line.) The first team to put three symbols in a straight line is the winner.

48 Pairs

Description The game 'Pairs' is known in England as Pelmanism, after a certain Pelman Institute. It forms the basis of commercially produced games in many countries. Players try to collect as many pairs of cards as possible. A pair is composed of two animal cards, two object cards, or two person cards.

Language	**Cards**
Animal, object, person.	all sets, mixed

Space Normal classroom.

Numbers Groups of 4–6 players, with 3 cards each.

Procedure

1 The leader shuffles the cards and places them face down on the table. Players cannot look at the cards.

2 Player 1 touches a card and guesses what it is, e.g. *Animal.*

3 He turns it over, and if it is an animal card, he touches another card and also says *Animal*. If he is right, he has won a pair of cards, which he keeps. He then tries to win another pair, as before. If a player does not guess a card correctly, the card is left where it was, face down, and then it is the turn of Player 2, and so on, around the group.

4 The game ends when all possible pairs have been made. The player with most pairs is the winner.

Variant 1

Play as above, except that the group is divided into two teams, with two or three players on each side.

 49

Paper aeroplane competition

Description Players win points by throwing paper aeroplanes.

Language	Cards/Materials
1 Revision of past lessons, e.g. Teacher: *What's the time? What colour's Joe's shirt? etc.* 2 Numbers.	1 piece of paper per child optionally:  any set(s)

Space A large classroom or the playground.

Numbers The whole class, as a team competition.

Procedure

1 Tell each player to make a paper aeroplane.
2 Divide the class into two teams and appoint a scorer for each team.
3 Stand the players at the back of the classroom, with one team on the left and the other on the right. The players hold their aeroplanes. Allow a minute or two for the players to test their aeroplanes.
4 Tell them they will get 10 points for their team if their aeroplanes go past a certain point, e.g. the front row. In addition, they will get extra points for hitting certain objects, e.g. 10 points for hitting the table, 50 for hitting a volunteer sitting on the table, 30 for hitting the blackboard (and perhaps extra points, e.g. 100 or more, for hitting a large target like a dartboard drawn on the board), and so on. Write this on the board: Table – 10 points, etc.
5 Ask the first player a question, e.g. *What's the time?* (Optionally, the question can refer to cards, e.g. *What's he doing?*). Tell him he can consult two friends.
6 If he answers correctly, say *O.K. Throw your aeroplane.* If he does not answer correctly, make him repeat the correct answer. He can then throw his aeroplane, but he must turn round and throw it over his shoulder.
7 The team with most points after everybody has thrown (or after 10 minutes) is the winner.

 50 Parrots

Description In this game, the pupils are 'parrots' and repeat what you say, but only if it is true.

Language	Cards
The lexis of the cards.	any set(s)

Space Normal classroom.

Numbers The whole class.

Procedure

1 Show the front of a card and make a statement about it, e.g. *It's a giraffe.*
2 If the statement is true, the pupils repeat it. If the statement is false, the pupils remain silent.
3 This game can be played for amusement only, with no scoring, or as a team competition (Variant 1).

Alternative language

Any true or false statements about children in the class e.g. Teacher: *Joe's wearing a red pullover.*

Variant 1

1 Divide the class into two teams.
2 Ask individuals in each team to respond, as in the basic game. Alternate between the teams.
3 Give one point for each correct response.
4 The first team to get five points is the winner.

Variant 2

Language	Materials
The alphabet.	

Write a letter of the alphabet on the board and say the letter (or another letter). Play as above. (If you say a different letter from the one on the board, name the letter correctly once or twice, so that the pupils learn the correct name.)

Variant 3

Language	Materials
Whose + possessives, e.g. Teacher: *Whose book is this?* Player X: *It's his/her/Sue's book.* or *It's his/hers/Sue's.*	

Procedure

1 Stand (12) players in front of the class, each holding an object, for (1 minute).

2 Send them back to their seats. Tell them to leave their objects on the table.

3 Stand a volunteer (Player X) in front of the class.

4 Hold up an object, e.g. a book, and ask the volunteer.

Teacher: *Whose book is this?* or
Whose is this book? or
Whose is this?

5 She replies, choosing between true and false statements:

It's his/her/Sue's book. or
It's his/hers/Sue's.

6 The class repeat this, if it is true.

Note: Any other true/false game can be used in the same way to practise the above possessives (see Index, true/false).

 **51 Party**

Description This is an adaptation of Happy Families. Players try to collect three pairs of cards. In this game a pair is composed of two cards showing the same object, e.g. the two chocolate cards.

Language	Cards
Requests, e.g. Player 1: *Have you got any chocolate?* Player X: *Yes, here you are,* or *No(, I haven't). (Sorry).*	Uncs.

Space Normal classroom.

Numbers The whole class, as a team competition.

Procedure

1 Divide the class into two teams. Explain that both teams are preparing food for a party. One team is going to make chocolate cakes and the other is going to make jam sandwiches. They are going to race to see who finishes first.

2 Give the chocolate cake team the following three cards: milk, chocolate and flour. Explain that a lot of children are coming to the party, and they have to make a very big cake. They have all the other ingredients, but they need more of the ingredients on their cards (in other words, they have to try to get the other three cards, making pairs as in Happy Families).

3 Give the jam sandwich team cards showing bread, jam and butter. Again, they have to try to get the other cards showing those ingredients.

4 Give the remaining twelve cards to three volunteers, four cards each.

5 Stand the three volunteers in different parts of the room. They represent 'neighbours' of the players. The players will ask them for the ingredients they need. Tell the three neighbours to hold the Jokers, but ignore them.

6 A team leader (Player 1), in consultation with the rest of the team, asks any one of his neighbours (Player X) for the card he needs, e.g.

Player 1: *Have you got any chocolate?*
Player X: *Yes, here you are.* or
No, I haven't.

7 If Player X has the card, she must give it to Player 1. (If Player X cheats by previously signalling that she has the card, declare the other team the winner, and start again.) Players who win cards make a pair, and carry on until they get three pairs, or are refused a card. If they are refused a card, it is the turn of the other team.

8 The first team to make three pairs is the winner.

Alternative language

Enough, much, more and some with uncountable nouns, e.g.
Player 1: *We haven't got enough/much chocolate. Can we have some more, please?*
Player X: *Yes, here you are.* or *I haven't got any (chocolate). (Sorry).*

 **52 Poker-face**

Description This is a new pair game which is especially flexible from the language point of view. A player makes a true or false statement about a card and tries to put on a neutral 'poker-face', so that the other player cannot see if he is telling the truth or not. The object of the game is to put all one's cards down on the table.

Language	Cards
Have got + the lexis of the cards, e.g. Player 1: *I've got a giraffe/an animal.* Player 2: *I (don't) believe you.*	any set(s)

Space Normal classroom.

Numbers This is really a game for 2 players, but pupils sometimes like to play it in groups. 3+ cards per player.

Procedure

1 Demonstrate with a pupil in the front row, with three cards each.

2 Players can look at their cards. They hold them in their left hand (if they are right-handed), and they show the back of the cards.

3 Player 1 chooses any card and holds it up in his right hand, still showing the back.

4 He then says, for example, *I've got a giraffe.* This may be true, and it may not.

5 Player 2 studies his face and says *I believe you.*, or *I don't believe you.*

6 Player 1 turns the card round, to show the front.

7 The next step depends on whether Player 2 'read' Player 1's face correctly when she said *I believe you.*, or *I don't believe you.* If she 'read' Player 1's face correctly, and was not deceived, then Player 2 puts down a card (any card). But if not, and she was deceived, then Player 1 puts down a card (any card).

8 It is then Player 2's turn to hold up a card and say *I've got...* Make sure that she holds the card up: children sometimes forget to do this.

9 Players take it in turns to hold up cards and say *I've got...*

10 The first player to put all his cards down on the table is the winner.

Alternative language

> Present progressive, e.g.
> Player 1: *I'm looking at a giraffe/an animal.*

Variant 1

The following variant may be useful for later use. Play as in the basic game, except that players do not alternate. If Player 1 holds up a card, and successfully deceives Player 2, he carries on holding up cards until he either wins or fails to deceive her.

Variant 2

Language	Cards
Request 'Can I have?' e.g. Player 2: *Can I have that orange, please?* Player 1: *Yes, here you are/. No (, you can't).*	any set(s)

Procedure

Play as in the basic game, except that:

1 Before playing, the two players show each other their cards.

2 When Player 1 holds up a card, Player 2 speaks first, e.g. *Can I have that orange, please?*

Variant 3

Language	Materials
Numbers: any numbers, cardinals (1, 2, 3, etc.) or ordinals (first, second, third, etc.)	Each child needs a few small pieces of paper on which to write numbers.

Procedure

Play as in the basic game, except that players use numbers written on small pieces of paper instead of cards. They conceal a piece of paper in their right hand, and hold it up, saying a number, e.g.
Player 1: *Fifteen.*
Player 2: *I (don't) believe you.*

Alternative language

> 1 Age, e.g. Player 1: *I'm nine (years old).*
>
> 2 Age with 'will', e.g. Player 1: *I'll be ten next year.*

Play with numbers on small pieces of paper, as in the previous variant. The number is imagined to be the player's true age at the time of speaking.
To practise *I'll be ten next year.*, players should be holding the previous number, in this case 9.

Variant 4

Language	Cards
I've got a/some, e.g.	
1 I've got a giraffe.	1 Sings., Places, Profs.
2 I've got some bread.	2 Uncs.
3 I've got some horses.	3 Plurals

Procedure

1 Take one of the above sets of cards (or a mixture of sets, to practise 'a' and 'some' together.) Shuffle the cards and put them in a pile face down on the table.
2 Divide the class into two teams, and appoint a scorer for each team.
3 A player from one team (Player 1) comes to the front of the class and picks up the top card. He shows the back of it.
4 He talks to any player in the other team (Player 2) and says e.g. *I've got a giraffe.*
5 Player 2 says *I believe you.*, or *I don't believe you.* If Player 2 is right, she gets a point for her team. If not, Player 1 gets a point for his team.
6 It is then the turn of the other team, and so on, with teams alternating.
7 The first team to get (3) points is the winner.

Variant 5

Language	Cards
How much? A lot of/Not much, e.g. Player 1: *I've got some bread.* Player 2: *How much bread have you got?* Player 1: *I've got a lot of bread./I haven't got much bread.* Player 2: *I (don't) believe you.*	Uncs.

Play as Variant 4 above, except that Player 1 is the first player to speak: *I've got some bread.* Put the dialogue on the board in the form of model sentences, as described in the Introduction, p. 4–5.

Alternative language

Language	Cards
How many? A lot of/Not many, e.g. Player 1: *I've got some horses.* Player 2: *How many horses have you got?* Player 1: *I've got ten horses./I've got a lot of horses./I haven't got many horses.*	Plurals

Two or three animals or objects are considered 'not many'. Six or more are considered 'a lot'.

Variant 6

Language	Cards
Invitations, e.g. Player 1: *Do you want to/Would you like to play football?* Player 2: *Yes, O.K./All right. No, thanks. (I'd rather play tennis).*	Verbs

Procedure

Play as Variant 4, for the whole class. Player 2 says *Yes* if she thinks Player 1 is holding the football card. She then mimes playing football.
If she thinks he is holding some other card she says *No, thanks.* Optionally she can say and mime a different activity, e.g. *I'd rather play tennis.*

Alternative language

Language	Cards
Suggestions, e.g. Player 1: *Shall we play football?/Let's play football.*	Verbs

Player 2 replies as in the previous language box, except that she does not say *Thanks* in reply to a suggestion.

53 Presents

Description This is a new game with some luck and some skill (memory). Players try to get the three cards they want, by asking other players for them.

Language	Cards
Revision of the lexis of the cards (spoken and written) + 'the', e.g. Player 1: *Have you got the car?* Player X: *Yes (, I have). Here you are./No (, I haven't). (Sorry).*	all sets, mixed

Space Normal classroom.

numbers Groups of 4 or 5 players with 3 cards each.

Procedure

1 Players sit in groups of four or five, with three cards each. They put all the cards together in the middle, face up.

2 Tell them to look at the cards. They each make a list of the three things that they would like as presents. If they cannot write the word, they can make a simple drawing. They do not show the other players their list. Obviously, several players may want the same present: that is part of the fun. If the Verbs and Professions sets are included, the players can imagine that they are pictures or toys.

3 The leader shuffles the cards and deals them. The players look at the front of the cards, and show the back.

4 The first player (Player 1) asks any other player (Player X) for a card he wants, e.g.

Player 1: *Have you got the car?*
Player X: *Yes, here you are.* or
No, I haven't.

If Player X has the card, she must give it to him. Player 1 takes the card and puts it with the others in his hand, showing the back of the card in the normal way. Explain that he has won it, but only for the moment, because another player may ask for it later. Player 1 then carries on asking for cards until he gets the three cards in his list, or is refused a card. If he is refused a card, it is the turn of the player who refused him.

5 The first player to get all three cards in his list is the winner.

Language	**Cards/Materials**
Any answers to questions put by the teacher. This includes, for example, **1** Revision of past lessons, e.g. Teacher: *How old are you? What's the time?* **2** All tenses of the verb.	2 dice a piece of chalk optional: any set(s)

Space Normal classroom.

Numbers The whole class, as a team competition.

Procedure

1 Mark nine different points around the classroom, and number them from 1 to 9, either on the walls or on the floor.

2 Divide the class into two teams. Select five representatives of each team and stand them in lines next to point number 1.

3 Give each team a name, e.g. Lions and Tigers, and give each line numbers from 1 to 5 (e.g. Lions 1, 2, etc.).

4 Tell Lions 1 to throw a dice and move forwards the number shown.

5 Ask Lions 1 a question. e.g. *How old are you?* (Optionally, the question can refer to cards, e.g. *What's he doing?*). If he answers correctly he stays at that point in the room; if he answers incorrectly he is replaced by another player from his team, but the new player goes back one number.

6 It is then the turn of Tigers 1, and so on, with the teams alternating.

7 The game ends when a player reaches the end. Two possible endings for dice games are given on p. 6–7 of the Introduction.

54 Rally

Description This is a new game in which players move forwards from one stage to the next, as in a car rally. This type of game is sometimes organized for children on visits to the countryside. At each stage the players are given a written instruction like 'Find 3 snails', and when they have carried it out they move on to the next stage.

55 Robot

Description This is a visually amusing game in which players imitate the movements of a robot.

Language	Materials
1 Imperatives: walk, touch, etc.	
2 Parts of the body: head, nose, etc.	
3 Adverbs of manner: slowly, quickly, etc.	
4 Adverbs of place: forwards, left, etc.	
Teacher: *Touch your nose and walk slowly. Take one step forwards.*	

Space Normal classroom, or the playground.

Numbers 2+ volunteers.

Procedure

1 Ask for two or more volunteers to be robots.
2 Give a series of orders for the robots to follow. The orders are accumulative: the robots do not stop one action when they start another. For example, Teacher: *Walk . . . . Open and shut your mouth . . . . Touch your right knee . . . Say 'I'm a robot'*, etc. Pupils enjoy replacing the teacher and thinking of difficult combinations of actions.

Variant 1

1 Do this as a team competition, choosing one pupil to represent each team.
2 One team wins if the other team's robot makes a mistake.

56 Ship in a fog

Description This is a mother-tongue game. A player guides a blindfolded player around obstacles.

Language	Materials
1 Imperatives.	a blindfold
2 Adverbs of place. Teacher: *Take one step forwards. Take two small steps to the left. Turn right. Stop.*	

Space An open area in the classroom.

Numbers 1 volunteer.

Procedure

1 Place two chairs to represent the port.
2 Put some obstacles on the way to port: chairs, pupils, etc.
3 Blindfold a volunteer.
4 Stand behind him. You are the 'Captain' and guide the blindfolded 'ship' into port, e.g. Captain: *Take one step forwards. . . . Take two small steps to the left. . . . Turn right. . . . Stop.*

5 Ask for a volunteer to replace you as Captain.

Variant

Language	Materials
As in the basic game.	2 blindfolds

Numbers 4 volunteers.

Procedure

1 Divide the class into two teams. Ask for two volunteers from each team.
2 Play as above, except that there is one Captain and one blindfolded ship from each team.
3 The first ship to enter port is the winner.

57 Simon says

Description This is perhaps the best known of all school games. The leader gives orders and the class follow them, but only if the orders are introduced by the phrase 'Simon says . . .'.

Language	Materials
Imperatives, e.g. Teacher: *Simon says, 'Stand up.'* *Sit down. Simon says, 'Touch your nose.' Touch your left ear. Simon says, 'Twiddle your thumbs.' Simon says, 'Nod your head.' Say hello.*	

Space Normal classroom, or the playground.

Numbers The whole class.

Procedure

1 Give a series of orders. The class follow them, but only if you first say 'Simon says . . .'.
   Teacher: *Simon says, 'Stand up.'* (The class stand up). *Sit down.* (Anyone who sits down is out).
2 The pupil left at the end is the winner, and can be leader.

Pupils get very good at this game, although the words left and right are useful for a time to get them out. The following variants may help:

Variant 1

Tell the pupils to play with their eyes shut. (This means that they cannot imitate each other).

Variant 2

Make misleading movements. For example, say *Simon says, 'Touch your nose.'*, and touch your ear.

Variant 3

Teacher: *Shall we play 'Simon says'?*
Class: *Yes!*
Teacher: *All right. Stand up.* Everyone stands up and everyone is out!

Variant 4

Language	Materials
Pronouns *Look at me/him/her/us/them.*	

Procedure

Stand volunteers around the room, and include the phrase *Look at me/him/her*, etc in the game as described.

It will be more difficult for the pupils if you do not point when you say, e.g. *Look at him.*

58 Simple arithmetic

Description Simple arithmetic makes a surprisingly popular team competition.

Language	Materials
Numbers and the language of simple arithmetic, e.g. Teacher: 1 *What's nine and/plus fourteen?* 2 *What's seven times nine?* 3 *What's thirty-nine divided by three?*	

Space Normal classroom.

Numbers The whole class, as a team competition.

Procedure

1 Divide the class into two teams and appoint a scorer in each team.
2 Ask players from alternate teams questions, e.g.
   Teacher: *What's nine and fourteen?*
   Player X: *Twenty-three.*
   If she wishes, Player X can consult the scorer before answering, and write the sum on the board, e.g. 9 + 14.
3 Give one point for each correct answer.
4 The team with most points after (10) minutes is the winner.

59 Spelling bee

Description A 'spelling bee' is simply a spelling competition, with points given for words correctly spelt.

Language	Materials
Spelling	

Space Normal classroom.

Numbers The whole class, as a team competition.

Procedure

1 Divide the class into two teams, and appoint a scorer for each team. If space permits it, stand the two teams in lines facing each other, and stand in the middle. If this is not possible, the players can remain in their seats.

2 Ask the first player (the player at the end of the line) to spell a word, e.g. cat. Start with easy words. The scorer writes the letters on the board as they are called out. If the player spells the word correctly, give a point to his team. If he makes a mistake, offer the word to the first player in the other team.

3 Traditionally, players who make mistakes are out, and go back to their seats: the last player standing is the winner. But to keep everybody in the game, give one point to the team that finishes the word correctly. The first team to get (5) points is the winner.

Variant 1

Language	Cards
The spelling of the lexis of the cards.	any set(s)

Procedure

Play as described in the basic game, but hold up a card instead of saying the word.

Variant 2

Play as in the basic game, except that the first player says the first letter of the word, the second player says the second, and so on. If a mistake is made, offer the word to the first player in the other team. Give one point for each correct letter.

Variant 3

Write a word on the board, but omitting the vowels, e.g. tbl. Pupils spell the complete word t-a-b-l-e, with either one word per pupil, or with one letter per pupil as in Variant 2. Rub out the previous consonants (tbl) when you put the next word on the board, so that the pupils do not learn the abbreviated form.

60 Spending competition

Description This is an adaptation of a foreign language game. Players try to spend as much money as possible.

Language	Cards/Materials
Money – pounds and pence, e.g. £3.50	1 dice per group. any set(s) 1 counter or coin per player, to mark his place.

Space Normal classroom.

Numbers Groups of 4 players, so far as possible, with 3 cards per player. (If this is not possible, groups of 3 players with 4 cards per player).

Procedure

1 Check that the players know the written form of English money (e.g. 'three pounds fifty' = £3.50) and can add up a column of figures, e.g.

£3.50
£2.80
_____
£6.30

2 Write the following on the board, for reference:

First round: 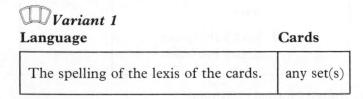 = 3 cards, £3.
Second round: ⚁ and ⚂ = 3 cards, £3.50.

3 Explain that the players have won a competition organized by a large department store. They can go round the store twice, buying as many things as they can, and the store will give them their money back later. In other words, they want to buy as many things as possible, especially expensive things. (If cards showing people are used, tell them to imagine that the card is a painting.)

50

4 Groups arrange 12 cards as shown:

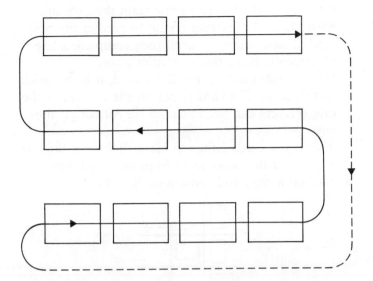

The first card is in the bottom row, on the left. Players move in the direction of the arrows.

5 The first player throws a dice, and moves forward the number shown. The number thrown also represents the money he can spend. Refer to the rules on the board: On the first round (the first time players go round) if a player throws a 3, he moves forward 3 cards, and can buy the third card for £3.

The second round is exactly the same, except that players throw twice: the second throw (e.g. 5) is multiplied by 10 and gives the number of pence (e.g. 50p), which is added on to the price of the card.

6 The leader of the group sells the card: *£3, please.*, and writes down what each player has spent. He can also participate himself. Players can pay:
a by handing over imaginary money.
b by writing the sum (e.g. £3.50) on a small piece of paper.
c by making the 'money' as needed on small pieces of paper; for example, £3.50 would be three 'notes' of £1 and one 'coin' of 50p.
d by using previously prepared imitation money.

7 When a player buys a card, that card is turned face down. Players who land on it cannot buy it; they must wait for their next turn.

8 Players move directly from the first round to the second. Cards which are face down are left face down.

9 The player who has spent most money when everyone has finished the second round is the winner.

61 Tallest

Description This is a simple game in which points are won for making true statements about pupils and objects in the classroom.

Language	Materials
Comparative and superlative adjectives, e.g. Player X: *I'm the tallest boy in the room.* Player Y: *(That's not true.) I'm/Joe's taller (than you).*	

Space Normal classroom.

Numbers The whole class, as a team competition.

Procedure

1 Divide the class into two teams.

2 A player from one team stands up and makes a statement containing a superlative, e.g. *I'm the tallest boy in the room.* If nobody disagrees, his team gets one point. It is then the turn of somebody in the other team. If somebody in the other team disagrees with a statement he can challenge by saying, for example, *I'm taller than you.*, or *Joe's taller than you.* Measure the two players and give a point to the player who was right.

3 Explain that words (e.g. tallest) can only be used three times. Then they must think of another word. The alternative language below may help them, if they are having difficulties.

4 The first team to get (10) points is the winner.

Alternative language

1 This/that is + comparatives/superlatives, e.g.
Player X: *This is the biggest book in the room.*
Player Y: *This book is bigger (than that one).*

2 Have got + comparatives/superlatives, e.g.
Player X: *I've got the biggest feet in the room.*
Player Y: *I've got/Joe's got bigger feet (than you).*

62
Three in a row

Description This is based on a game which is popular in many countries, in one form or another. In Spain it is called 'Tres en Raya' and takes the form of a board game with counters. In England it is played with pencil and paper and is called Noughts and Crosses (see Noughts and Crosses on the Board, p. 41). Two players take it in turns to put their symbol – a nought (0) or a cross (X) – in the squares shown below. The player who puts three symbols in a straight line wins. In the version described below, the symbols have been replaced by cards.

Language	**Cards/Materials**
Animal, object, person.	Blu-tack to attach the cards to the board (see Introduction, p. 7). 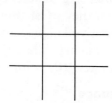all sets, mixed

Space Normal classroom.

Numbers Groups of 4 players, with 9 cards per group. (Groups of 3 players with 9 cards per group are also possible).

Procedure

1 Draw the following parallel lines on the board.

2 Explain that this is a pair game. The winner is the player who puts three cards in a straight line: vertically, horizontally, or diagonally.

3 Ask four volunteers to come to the front of the class, to demonstrate the game. Divide them into two teams and appoint a leader in each team.

4 One of the leaders shuffles the cards and places them face down in a pile in the centre. Players cannot look at the cards.

5 The first player tries to predict if the top card is animal, object or person. He says, e.g. *Animal.* He then turns it over. If it is an animal, he puts it in one of the squares on the board. (He can put it in any square he wishes, but the strongest square is the centre square, and it is normal to put it

there.) He should put the card horizontally (the other team will put its cards vertically, to distinguish them). The same team then continues, with Player 1's partner trying to predict the next card. Teams carry on until they complete a line of three cards, or fail to predict a card.

When a team fails to predict a card, it is the other team's turn. The card is put on the bottom of the pile. Players can say *Put it on the bottom.*, if they wish.

Teams use cards either to make their own line, or to prevent the other team from making theirs.

6 The game may end something like this:

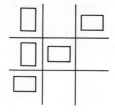

In this example, the team with the horizontal cards wins, because they have made a straight line.

7 Tell the class to play in groups, and give out the cards. Groups can draw the parallel lines on a piece of paper, or mark them on the table or floor with chalk, or imagine them (see Variant below).

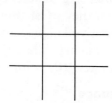*Variant*

If players imagine the parallel lines, the game is a little more complex, because a line of cards may go in a direction that some of the players had not thought of. But the rule is simple: you cannot have more than three cards in a straight line.

63
True/false chairs

Description In this game the leader makes a statement and players run to a chair marked TRUE or to another chair marked FALSE.

Language	**Cards**
The lexis of the cards.	any set(s)

Space The basic game probably requires the whole classroom, or the playground. Variant 1 requires less space.

Numbers The whole class, as a team competition.

Procedure

1 Place two chairs together in the middle of the blackboard and write TRUE above one and FALSE above the other. Alternatively, place two chairs in any open area and write the words on the floor with chalk.

2 Divide the class into two teams, and appoint a scorer in each team.

3 Stand the teams an equal distance from the chairs. Give the players in each team numbers:

TRUE   FALSE

 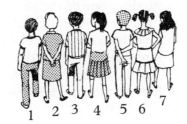

7 6 5 4 3 2 1   1 2 3 4 5 6 7

4 Hold up a card and name an animal or object, followed by a number, e.g. *An orange . . . Number 4!* If the card does show an orange, the two number fours run to be the first to sit on the TRUE chair. If it does not show an orange, they run to the FALSE chair.

5 Give one point each time a player sits on the correct chair.

6 When the player is sitting on the chair, hold up the card again and ask *What is it?* Give another point for the correct answer. If the card does show an orange, the player simply repeats *(It's) an orange.* If the card does not show an orange, he will have to name it correctly, e.g. *(It's) an elephant.*

7 The team with most points after 10 minutes (or when the cards have been used, or when every player has had a turn) is the winner.

Alternative language

Language	Cards
Tenses of the verb, e.g. Present progressive: Teacher: *He's swimming.*	Verbs

Variant 1

Language	Cards
Any true or false statements, e.g. Teacher: *Joe's wearing a red pullover.* *Spiders have ten legs.*	

Procedure

Play as the basic game, but instead of using cards, make statements about things in the classroom: *Joe's wearing a red pullover.*, *It's three o'clock.*, etc. Another possibility is to prepare a list of true and false statements based on a textbook for another subject: *Spiders have ten legs, Paris is the capital of Germany,* etc.

Variant 2

If space is a problem, choose (5) representatives of each team. When each representative has had his turn, he returns to his seat. When all (5) have had their turn, add up the total of points won by each team, and give an extra point to the winner. Then start again with (5) new representatives. Add their total of points won to the previous total. Stop the game after playing it (4) times. The team with most points is the winner.

Variant 3

Place a chair in the middle between two teams. One team is the TRUE team, and responds to true statements; the other is the FALSE team, and responds to false statements. Draw a chalk line on the floor in front of each team.

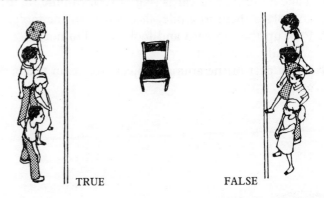

TRUE   FALSE

Play as in the basic game, except that if a statement is true, only the player from the TRUE team crosses the line and sits on the chair. He can do this slowly – there is no hurry in this version. Wait (5) seconds before saying if a player has moved correctly or not. Players who cross the line in error lose a point. Players who should have crossed the line and gone to the chair, but have not, also lose a point.

64 Unfinished drawings

Description In this game, players see an incomplete drawing, and try to guess what it represents.

Language	Materials
Any lexis.	

Space Normal classroom.

Numbers The whole class.

Procedure

1 Draw part of an animal, object, etc. on the board.
2 Ask the class to guess what it is: *What's this/that?* or *What is it?*
3 If nobody guesses, add something to the drawing, and so on, until it is guessed.
4 When it is guessed, finish it quickly.
5 The player who guessed it replaces you, and does his own drawing for the class to guess.

 Variant

Language	Cards
The lexis of the cards.	any set(s)

Procedure

1 Take a number of cards (e.g. a set). Shuffle them, and place them in a pile, face down on the table.
2 Pick up the top card and look at it. Do not let anybody else see it.
3 Draw part of the animal, object etc., as in the basic game.

65 What a nice cat!

Description This is a simple game based on finding adjectives.

Language	Cards
What a + adjective + noun, e.g.	
1 *What a nice cat!*	1 Sings., Places, Verbs, Profs.
2 *What nice bread!*	2 Uncs.
3 *What nice cats!*	3 Plurals

Space Normal classroom.

Numbers The whole class, as a team competition.

Procedure

1 Divide the class into two teams.
2 Take (18) cards, shuffle them and put them in a pile face down on the table.
3 Pick up the top card and show it to one of the teams. Tell them they have (20 seconds) to produce one of the above phrases. If they can produce a sentence that makes reasonable sense, give them the card. If they cannot produce a sentence, offer it to the other team. Adjectives can only be used once in the same game.
4 The team that wins most cards is the winner.

66 Winner says M

Description In this game, players recite the alphabet, saying one or two letters each. The winner is the player who says the letter M.

Language	Materials
The alphabet, from A to M.	

Space Normal classroom.

Numbers A pair game.

Procedure

1 Explain that players can say one or two letters of the alphabet, but not three. The winner is the player who says M.

2 Demonstrate with a player in the class, e.g.
Teacher: *AB*. (Explain that the player can say C
or CD)
Player: *CD*.
Teacher: *E*. Player: *F*.
Teacher: *GH*. Player: *I*.
Teacher: *J*. Player *KL*.
Teacher: *M*.
(The teacher won this game at the point where he
said J. Players who say the letter fourth from the
end – in this case, J – will win. Do not tell the
class this!)
3 Tell the class to play in pairs.

Alternative language

1 Numbers, e.g. 1 to 15. Also ordinals, e.g. first
  to fifteenth.

2 Days of the week: the winner says the last day.

3 Months of the year: the winner says December.

67 Word chain

Description This is a memory game. Each player
names all the animals, objects, etc. which have
previously been named, and adds one of his own.

Language	Materials
Lexical sets, e.g. animals	

Space Normal classroom.

Numbers The whole class, as a team competition.

Procedure

1 Divide the class into two teams. Tell a player
  from one team to name, for example, an animal:
  Player X: *Elephant*.

2 Tell a player from the other team to repeat the
  word, and add another, e.g. Player Y: *Elephant,
  lion*. Include the weaker learners near the
  beginning to make it easier for them.

3 Carry on in this way, alternating between the
  teams. Keep a record of the animals named, to
  check for mistakes. When a mistake is made, give
  one point to the other team, and start again.

4 The first team to get (3) points wins.

Alternative language

1 I'm thinking of an elephant, a tiger . . .

2 I can see a book, a blackboard, . . .

Variant 1
Language

Language	Materials
Imperatives, e.g. *Touch your nose, nod your head, (don't) say hello.*	

Procedure

Play as in the basic game, except that a volunteer in
front of the class performs the actions – or does not
perform them, in the case of the negative.

Variant 2
Language

Language	Materials
Narrative and connectors (then, and, after that, etc.) e.g. *I wake up at half past seven. Then I switch the light on. After that I get up, go to the bathroom and have a wash . . .*	

Procedure

1 Describe your daily routine (for the simple
  present), miming and speaking: *I wake up at half
  past seven.*, etc.

2 Stop after (3) sentences and ask a player to repeat
  what you have said, also miming and speaking.

3 Add another sentence, and so on, as in the basic
  game.

Variant 3
Language

Language	Materials
Simple past of see: Joe: *I can see a book.* Sue: *Joe saw a book, and I can see a chair.* Dave: *Joe saw a book, Sue saw a chair and I can see . . .*	

Procedure

Play as in the basic game, except that previous
players have to be named: *Joe saw a book.*, etc.

Games for Younger Learners (aged approximately 3–6)

This section gives ten games played by younger children in the mother tongue. They cover simple items like numbers and colours. In addition to the games given below, some of the simpler games in this book can also be used. The obvious games are those with a physical response, like *Bring me a pen*, *Giant steps and fairy steps*, *Simon says* and *Robot*. Another possibility is *Blindfolded conversation*.
If you have a very small class (e.g. 3 or 4 children), it is worth trying some of the more complicated games, such as the 'animal-object-person' games, like *Memory*. A list is given in the index, under 'animal-object-person'.

68 Blind man's buff

Description A blindfolded child tries to catch the other players.

Language	Materials
Players: *Here I am!* 'Blind man': *Got you!*	chalk to draw a circle on the floor a blindfold

Space An open area in the classroom, or the playground.

Numbers The whole class.

Procedure
1 Draw a circle on the floor and stand the class in it.
2 Blindfold a child and tell him to catch someone.
3 Tell the others to go near him, saying *Here I am!*
4 When the 'blind man' catches someone he says *Got you!* (meaning 'I've got you!') and hands him the blindfold. Players who step outside the circle also become the 'blind man'.

69 Cops and robbers

Description Players try to pick up an object and run back to safety without being touched.

Language	Materials
The lexis of classroom objects.	any small objects a piece of chalk

Space An open area in the classroom, or the playground.

Numbers The whole class.

Procedure
1 Divide the children into two groups: Cops (i.e. policemen) and Robbers.
2 Stand the groups behind lines, facing each other.
3 Put objects on the ground, about a third of the way from the Robbers to the Cops.
4 When you shout out the name of an object, the Robbers run and try to pick it up and take it back across their line. If the Cops touch them before they cross their line they have to return the object.

70 First shout

Description Players try to be the first to shout out the name of an animal, object, etc.

Language	Cards
The lexis of the cards.	any set(s)

Space Normal classroom.

Numbers The whole class.

Procedure
1 Sit the children in a row or rows.
2 Tell a child (Player 1) to walk up and down the rows, and stop behind any child (Player X).
3 Show a card.

4 The two children shout out the name of the animal, object, etc. on the card. If Player 1 shouts first, then Player X is out, and Player 1 continues. If Player X shouts first, then she replaces Player 1.

71 Fox

Description A child chases another round a circle.

Language	Materials
Fox: *Can I come in?* *When can I come in?* *At (six) o'clock.*	a piece of chalk

Space An open area in the classroom, or the playground.

Numbers The whole class.

Procedure
1. Stand the children in a circle holding hands. One child is a rabbit; he is inside the circle. Another child is the fox; he is outside the circle and wants to get in.
2. The fox taps somebody (Player X) on the shoulder and says:
   Fox: *Can I come in?*
   Player X: *No (, you can't).*
   Fox: *When (can I come in)?*
   Player X: *At (6) o'clock.*
3. All the children in the circle then count: one o'clock, two o'clock, etc. until they get to six o'clock. They then lift their arms and the fox enters the circle. He chases the rabbit out of it, and around the outside.
4. The rabbit is safe if he goes around three times (from the point he left the circle) without being caught. If he does this, he joins the circle, and the fox starts again, with another rabbit in the middle. If the rabbit is caught, he becomes the new fox, and the old fox joins the circle.

72 Good morning, Mr Jones!

Description Two players try to get to one empty seat.

Language	Materials
Good morning, Mr Jones!	

Space An open area in the classroom, or the playground.

Numbers The whole class.

Procedure
1. Sit the children on the ground in a circle.
2. One child stands up and walks around the outside of the circle.
3. He stops and says to any other child *Good morning, Mr Jones!*
4. The two children then run around the circle in opposite directions. When they meet they shake hands and say to each other *Good morning, Mr Jones!* They then carry on running to see who gets back to the empty seat first.
5. The child who is left standing then starts again.

73 Groups of five!

Description This is an elimination game: children who cannot form part of a group of (five) players are out.

Language	Materials
Low numbers, e.g. 1 to 10.	

Space An open area in the classroom, or the playground.

Numbers The whole class.

Procedure
1. Tell the children to move around in a circle, perhaps singing.
2. Shout *Groups of five!* The class form groups of five, and those who cannot form a group are out.
3. Repeat this, varying the number, e.g. *Groups of three!* until there are only (3) children left. They are the winners.

74 How many teeth, Mr Bear?

Description This is a chasing game. When Mr Bear is angry the children must all run home quickly.

Language	Materials
How many teeth, Mr Bear?	a piece of chalk

Space An open area in the classroom, or the playground.

Numbers The whole class.

Procedure

1 Choose a child to be 'Mr Bear'. Sit him in the middle of a large circle drawn on the floor.
2 Children enter the circle and ask Mr Bear *How many teeth, Mr Bear?*
3 Mr Bear gives a bad-tempered answer in a low voice. If he says any number except twenty, they are safe. But if he says *Twenty – very sharp!* they must all run home quickly. If he catches one of them in the circle, that child becomes Mr Bear.

75 Jacob, where are you?

Description Two children are blindfolded. One tries to catch the other, who tries to avoid being caught.

Language	Materials
Where are you? *Here I am. / I'm here.*	

Space An open area in the classroom, or the playground.

Numbers The whole class.

Procedure

1 Blindfold two children, 'Jacob' and his 'mother'.
2 Mother says *Jacob, where are you?*
3 Jacob replies *Here!* or *Here I am!* or *I'm here, Mummy!*
4 Mother tries to catch him – but he avoids her when he hears her coming, because he wants to hide.

Variant

A child looks for his cat: *Puss, puss, where are you?* The cat answers *Miaow!*

76 Noah's Ark

Description This is a miming game. Children try to guess which animal is being mimed.

Language	Materials
1 Animal lexis. 2 Identifying yourself, e.g. Mr and Mrs Noah: *Who are you?* Wife: *We're Mr and Mrs . . .*	

Space An open area in the classroom, or the playground.

Numbers The whole class.

Procedure

1 Choose two children to be Mr and Mrs Noah. Stand them at the door of the ark.
2 Take half the class (the boys, in a mixed class) aside and ask them to tell you what animal they are going to be. When they have all chosen a different animal, take them back and give them 'wives'. Do not tell the wives which animals they are.
3 The first couple go to the ark. Mr and Mrs Noah ask the wife *Who are you?*
4 The wife looks at her husband, who mimes the animal, and the wife answers, e.g. *We're Mr and Mrs Giraffe.* If she is right, they both go into the ark. If she is wrong, they are both drowned in the flood!

77 Out!

Description This is a game of 'touch'. Players who are touched are out.

Language	Materials
Colours	

Space An open area in the classroom, or the playground.

Numbers The whole class.

Procedure

1 Choose a child to be 'it'. Tell the others to run about while 'it' stands still.
2 Tell 'it' to call out a colour, e.g. *Red!*
3 He then chases anybody who is not wearing anything of that colour.
4 When he catches somebody he shouts *Out!*
5 Children who are out stand together in a group holding hands. They can all re-enter the game if a child who is not out goes between the legs of any of them.

Index to the language of the games

Entries are given in order of usefulness, where appropriate; otherwise in alphabetical order.

like
a) verb: see *My father likes apples; Do you like your neighbours?*;
b) verb (offering): see *Left, right and centre*, Variant; *Poker-face*, Variant 6, Alternative language;
c) preposition: see *Mother Magee is coming to stay.*

live see *Blindfolded conversation*, Alternative language; *My name's Joe.*

lot (a lot of) see *Kim's game with dice*, Variant 3; *Poker-face*, Variant 5; *Poker-face*, Variant 5, Alternative language.

many see under **how many?, not many.**

may I? see under **can I?**

modal verbs see *Front of the card*, Variant 6.

money see *Auction; Spending competition.*

months see *Winner says M*, Alternative language; see also *Do you like your neighbours?*, Alternative language; *Jumping the line*, Variant 2.

more see *Party*, Alternative language; *Happy families*, Variant 2.

Mr, Mrs see *Noah's Ark* (Younger Learners).

much see under **how much?, not much.**

must see *Front of the card*, Variant 6.

name see *Blindfolded conversation*, Alternative language; *My name's Joe.*

narrative see *Busy weekend; Kim's game around the room*, Variant; *Do you like your neighbours?*, Variant; *Funniest story; Word chain*, Variant 2.

nationalities see *Map game.*

not many, not much see *Kim's game with dice*, Variant 3; *Party*, Alternative language; *Poker-face*, Variant 5; *Poker-face*, Variant 5, Alternative language.

noun for games with uncountable (mass) and plural nouns see under **some/any.**

noun + noun see *Giant steps and fairy steps.*

numbers see *Bingo; Simple arithmetic; Father Carbasser; Paper aeroplane competition; Poker-face*, Variant 3; *Winner says M*, Alternative language; see also

Battleships; Dance of the ostriches; Earth, air and sea; Giant steps and fairy steps; Jumping the line, Variant 2; *Moors and Christians; Noughts and crosses on the board; Groups of five* (Younger Learners).

'object' see under **'animal-object-person' games.**

offers
a) offering to do something: see *Can I do it?*, Alternative language;
b) offering an object: see *Left, right and centre.*

one (pronoun) see *Happy families; Tallest.*

only see *Do you like your neighbours?*, Variant 1, Alternative language.

ordinals see *Winner says M*, Alternative language; *Poker-face*, Variant 3.

past progressive see *Mime*, Variant 3; see also under **narrative**, especially *Kim's game around the room*, Variant.

permission, asking see *Can I do it?*.

'person' see under **'animal-object-person' games.**

personal description see *My name's Joe.*

playground games see *Dance of the ostriches; Earth, air and sea; Fish; Giant steps and fairy steps; Hat game; Jumping the line; Moors and Christians; Robot; Simon says; True/False chairs;* and Games for Younger Learners.

possession see under **have (got).**

possessives see *Mine!; Fish*, Alternative language; *Parrots*, Variant 3.

post-modification see *Draw a man*, Alternative language.

preference see *Poker-face*, Variant 6.

prepositions of place see *Draw a man*, Variant; see also *Kim's game around the room.*

present continuous see under **present progressive.**

present perfect see *Hat game*, Variant 3.

present perfect progressive see *Coffeepotting.*

present progressive see *Hat game; Mime*, Variants 4 and 5; *Poker-face*, Alternative language; *Do you like your neighbours?*, Variant 2; *True/False chairs*, Alternative language; *True/False chairs*, Variant 1; *Front of the card*; see also *Coffeepotting; Giant steps and*

fairy steps, Variant; *Guess*, Alternative language; *House*, Variant 1; *I spy*, Alternative language; *Word chain*, Alternative language.

pronouns (demonstrative) see under **this/that.**

pronouns (personal, object)
a) verb + direct object: see *Simon says*, Variant 4;
b) verb + indirect object + direct object; see *Bring me a pen; Bring me a pen*, Variant 1;
c) verb + direct object + indirect object; see *Bring me a pen*, Variants 2 and 3.

pronouns (personal, subject) see the section on Revision Games on p. 8 of the Introduction.

pronouns (possessive) see *Mine!*

pronouns see also under **one; some/any.**

quantities see under **how many?, how much?, lot, not many, not much**; for weights (100g etc.) see *Foreign shopper.*

rather see *Poker-face*, Variant 6.

requests
a) requesting an object: see under **can I have**;
b) requesting permission to do something: see under **can I?**
c) requesting somebody to do something: see under **can you?**

revision games see *Fish; Moors and Christians; Noughts and crosses on the board; Paper aeroplane competition; Rally.*

right see under **left.**

rooms of a house see *House.*

shall I? (offer) see *Can I do it?*, Alternative language.

shall we? (suggestion) see *Poker-face*, Variant 6.

shopping see *Foreign shopper.*

should see *Front of the card*, Variant 6.

simple past see *Mime*, Variant 3; *Busy weekend; Do you like your neighbours?*, Variant 1, Alternative language; *Funniest story; Kim's game around the room*, Variant; *Word chain*, Variants 2 and 3; see also *Chang, Cheng, Ching, Chong, Chung; Coffeepotting; Father Carbasser; Front of the card*, Variant 6; *I spy*, Alternative language.

simple present
a) habit: see *Coffeepotting; Mime*, Variant 1; *Word Chain*, Variant 2; *Funniest story*; see

also *Blindfolded conversation,
Alternative language; Map
game.*

b) state: see *Bluff; Do you like
your neighbours?; My father
likes apples; Left, right and
centre,* Variant; *Poker-face.*

some see *Kim's game with dice,*
Variant 2; *Poker-face,* Variant 4.

some/any see *Happy families,*
Variant 2; *Happy families,* Variant
2, Alternative language; *Party;
Party,* Alternative language; see
also *Busy weekend.*

something see *I spy; Giant steps and
fairy steps,* Variant.

spelling see *Spelling bee; First letter.*

sport see *My name's Joe;* as lexical
set see *Earth, air and sea; Jumping
the line,* Variant 2.

suggestions see *Poker-face,* Variant
6.

superlatives see *Fish; Tallest.*

that see under **this.**

the see *Kim's game around the room;*
Presents; for omission of 'the' see
My father likes apples.

there (over there) see *Kim's game
around the room; Do you like your
neighbours?,* Variant 1.

there is/are see *House,* Alternative
language and Variant 2; *Kim's
game with dice,* Variants 2 and 3.

these see under **this.**

this/that (pronoun) see *Jumping the
line,* Variant 3 and 4; *Front of the
card,* Variant 5; *Hat game,* Variant
1; *Mine!; Unfinished drawing.*

this/that (determiner) see *Tallest,*
Alternative language; *Foreign
shopper; House.*

those see under **this.**

time see *Clock;* see also *Fox*
(Younger Learners).

to (from . . . to) see *Father Carbasser.*

true/false games see *Jumping the
line; Parrots; True/False chairs;
True/False chairs,* Variant 3.

want see *Left, right and centre,*

Variant; *Poker-face,* Variant 6.

weights see *Foreign shopper.*

wh- questions see *Coffeepotting.*

what? see *Front of the card; Guess.*

what (+ adj. + noun) see *What a
nice cat!*

when? see *Coffeepotting.*

where? see *Coffeepotting; Map game;
House,* Variant 1; see also *Jacob,
where are you?* (Younger Learners).

which one? see *Kim's game around
the room.*

who? see *House,* Variant 1;
Coffeepotting; see also *Noah's Ark*
(Younger Learners).

whose? see *Parrots,* Variant 3.

why? see *Coffeepotting.*

will a) future: see *Poker-face,*
Variant 3, Alternative
language;

b) offering: see *Can I do it?,*
Alternative language.

writing see *Front of the card,*
Variant 4; *Mime,* Variant 2.